From Stagnation to Acceleration

A Manifesto for Technological Advancement

by
Cornel Jefferson

Cornel Jefferson

Copyright 2024 Cornel Jefferson. All Rights reserved. No part of this publication may be reproduced without consent of the author.

"The real problem is not whether machines think but whether men do."

- B. F. Skinner

Cornel Jefferson

From Stagnation To Acceleration

Table of Contents

Introduction

Chapter 1: The Complacency Crisis

Chapter 2: The Rise of Effective Accelerationism

Chapter 3: The Fallacy of Degrowth

Chapter 4: Unleashing Technological Titans

Chapter 5: Embracing the Kardashev Ambition

Chapter 6: The Power of Bold Entrepreneurship

Chapter 7: Reimagining the Future of Work

Chapter 8: Technological Solutions to Global Challenges

Chapter 9: Fostering a Pro-Progress Culture

Chapter 10: Accelerating Towards a Limitless Future

Conclusion

Introduction

In a world teetering on the brink of unprecedented challenges, our collective future hangs in the balance. Climate change, resource scarcity, and social inequality loom large, threatening to derail human progress. Yet, amidst these daunting obstacles, a beacon of hope emerges: technology. The power to reshape our world lies at our fingertips, but are we bold enough to seize it?

"From Stagnation to Acceleration" is more than just a book; it's a rallying cry for a new era of human potential. We stand at a crossroads, faced with a choice between complacency and ambition. The path of least resistance beckons, tempting us to cling to outdated ideologies and fear-driven policies. But there is another way – a path of courage, innovation, and relentless progress.

Effective Accelerationism isn't just a theory; it's a blueprint for a brighter future. By harnessing the transformative power of technology, we can tackle our greatest challenges head-on. Imagine a world where clean energy powers our cities, where artificial intelligence revolutionizes healthcare, and where space exploration opens up new frontiers for humanity.

This manifesto is a call to action for individuals, businesses, and governments alike. It's time to shed our hesitation and embrace the extraordinary potential that lies within our grasp. The chapters that follow will challenge your assumptions, ignite your imagination, and arm you with the knowledge to become a catalyst for change.

Are you ready to abandon stagnation and accelerate towards a future limited only by our collective ambition? The journey begins now. Let's shape tomorrow, today.

Cornel Jefferson

Chapter 1: The Complacency Crisis

The Mirage of Modern Progress

In our fast-moving world, it's easy to get caught up in the bright and shiny lure of new technology. We look at our sleek smartphones, scrolling through social media filled with snapshots of our friends' highlight reels, all while asking a virtual assistant to help us with tasks. With all this convenience right at our fingertips, it's tempting to believe we're truly making progress, that we're living in a time of innovation that will lead us to a brighter tomorrow. But here's the catch: could it be that we are just experiencing the mirage of modern progress? An illusion that keeps us distracted from more serious issues, causing us to settle into complacency instead of sparking real change?

The phrase "mirage of modern progress" captures this idea perfectly. It suggests that what looks like advancement might just be smoke and mirrors, making us think we're moving forward when we might actually be going nowhere or, even worse, moving backward. Take smartphones, for example. These little devices have completely changed the way we connect, find information, and do business. In just a few seconds, we can chat with someone on the other side of the globe, shoot off an email, or look up a dinner recipe. But despite these perks, smartphones have also given rise to a number of social issues—like loneliness, shorter attention spans, and widening income gaps.

While our gadgets get fancier, the social problems they were supposed to solve hang around stubbornly. The platforms designed to bring us together often end up isolating us instead, creating echo chambers that amplify divisive conversations instead of fostering understanding. Think about social media, which is sold to us as a revolutionary way to connect and build community. Yet, studies show that people who spend a lot of time on social media often feel lonelier than those who don't. The irony is hard to ignore: the more we use these tools that claim to draw us closer, the more we seem to drift apart.

Automation offers another clear example of this mirage. Robots can accomplish tasks faster and more efficiently than people, signaling a move toward a more productive future. However, this efficiency often comes at a price. Entire job sectors get turned upside down, leaving many workers struggling to keep up in a fast-changing job market. While some industries flourish thanks to automation, others face the frightening reality of becoming obsolete. Instead of bringing everyone together for a shared vision of prosperity, technology can deepen existing divides and create a future filled with uncertainty for those left behind.

Looking back through history, we see that real technological revolutions have brought about major societal changes. The Industrial Revolution, for instance, was a time of incredible innovation—mass production, steam engines, and new ways to travel transformed economies and living conditions. But it also led to huge problems, like worker exploitation and environmental harm, which called for big changes and reforms. In contrast, many of the advancements we see today feel more like small tweaks rather than groundbreaking shifts. The question stands: are we really innovating, or just shuffling things around as if we were rearranging deck chairs on the Titanic?

To highlight this point, let's think about transportation. The shift from horse-drawn carriages to cars was a game-changer, reshaping cities and society itself. Today, however, developments like ride-sharing apps might seem revolutionary, but they only scratch the surface of deeper issues like traffic jams, pollution, and the economic factors affecting how we get around. Instead of tackling these bigger problems, we're left with a digital solution that, while convenient, doesn't address the core challenges we face.

Healthcare technology follows the same pattern. Yes, telemedicine has made it easier for patients to connect with doctors, but it doesn't solve the underlying problem of healthcare inequality that exists in many communities. Just because we can have a doctor's appointment over video doesn't mean everyone has equal access to the internet or the necessary technology. Even the most advanced medical devices and treatments often fail to reach the people who need them the most.

As we look around at the world of modern technology, we should ask ourselves: what does progress really mean? Is it just about shiny devices and apps that change our daily lives? Or is it about creating real change that breaks down the barriers we face as a society? The answer lies in our willingness to engage with these questions instead of settling for surface-level advancements that ignore the root causes of our challenges.

The reality is that while we're surrounded by amazing technology, it's the deeper innovations that can truly reshape our world for the better. We need to move past the mirage of modern progress, where flashy gadgets and headlines distract us from tackling the urgent issues of our time, like inequality, climate change, and social justice. Real progress calls for awakening, action, and a commitment to transforming society fundamentally.

Only by recognizing the limits of where we are now can we work towards a future that embraces meaningful innovation. It's time to peel back the layers of this illusion of progress and awaken the spirit of innovation that lies within us all. By doing so, we can not only navigate our current challenges more effectively but also build a future that is not just tech-savvy but also fair, sustainable, and full of promise.

The Consequences of Inaction

Today's world is a colorful mix of technologies and innovations that promise us convenience, productivity, and endless possibilities for the future. But underneath this shiny exterior lies a serious issue: the consequences of doing nothing. While we scroll through our social media feeds and admire the latest gadgets, industries are struggling, jobs are disappearing, and our ecosystems are on the verge of collapse. Complacency, that tempting pull toward inertia, can set off a chain reaction of problems that affect everyone. It's in this struggle between taking action and doing nothing that we uncover some of the most important lessons of our time.

Take the story of Blockbuster, for instance. Once a giant in video rentals, the company had more than 9,000 stores worldwide, ruling the market like a king. But when digital streaming came onto the scene, Blockbuster chose to ignore it. They scoffed at innovation, convinced their physical stores were unbeatable. Meanwhile, a small startup called Netflix was quietly changing how people enjoyed entertainment. As Blockbuster held onto its stores, Netflix embraced online streaming long before it became the norm. The outcome? Blockbuster filed for bankruptcy in 2010, while Netflix surged to over 200 million subscribers globally. The message is clear: when innovation knocks, ignoring it can lead to a dramatic downfall.

Kodak's story is another powerful reminder of what happens when a company fails to see change coming. Once a key player in photography, Kodak was known for film and had a place in countless homes, capturing memories for generations. However, a creeping paralysis set in as they invented the digital camera but didn't take advantage of it, fearing it would hurt their profitable film business. Instead of adapting to the digital age, they held on tight to their old ways—until it was too late. By the time Kodak finally tried to make a change, they were overwhelmed by the digital photography wave that had surged ahead without them. In 2012, Kodak went bankrupt, marking a shocking fall for a company that once led the charge in innovation. Their failure serves as a warning: refusing to embrace change can lead to extinction.

    The tales of Blockbuster and Kodak highlight the consequences of inaction that reach far beyond the business world. These issues touch on social and economic factors that affect individuals and communities alike. Job loss has become a major concern in this stagnant landscape. Companies are increasingly turning to automation and artificial intelligence to boost efficiency, but while they enjoy higher profits, workers are left struggling. For instance, manufacturers are automating assembly lines, cutting back on human labor. This shift toward automation has cost millions of jobs, leaving many people without the skills needed to adapt to a changing job market.

This creates a worrying cycle of growing inequality. The gap in technological access means some people are reaping the benefits of a tech-driven economy while others are left behind. This divide not only impacts jobs but also access to resources and opportunities. Those without the means or ability to learn new skills often find themselves in tough situations. A 2021 report showed that nearly 40% of jobs in the United States are at high risk of being automated in the next 20 years. The consequences are staggering, as entire communities face economic struggles while a few thrive. The divide between those who can adjust to change and those who cannot continues to widen, creating feelings of frustration and despair.

The environmental fallout from inaction is just as disturbing. As businesses prioritize quick profits over sustainable practices, our planet pays the price. Climate change is no longer a distant worry; it is an urgent reality. The hesitation to move toward renewable energy and sustainable practices reflects humanity's failure to act despite overwhelming evidence. Forests are cut down for sprawling developments, oceans are suffocated with plastic, and wildlife faces extinction—all while time runs out for us to make a change. The latest report from the Intergovernmental Panel on Climate Change (IPCC) warns that we have less than a decade to prevent catastrophic climate change, yet many industries are slow to respond.

The statistics highlight how urgent this issue is. According to the World Economic Forum, the global economy could lose up to $23 trillion by 2050 if we fail to take strong action against climate change. Inaction isn't just a personal choice; it's a collective threat that endangers our future. The warnings from scientists and activists urge us to wake up and take notice. Our shared inaction today could shape the future for generations to come.

The lessons from these cautionary tales are crystal clear: complacency is a risky game. The stories of Blockbuster and Kodak may seem like isolated events, but they reflect a larger problem in society. The intertwined issues of job loss, growing inequality, and environmental decline reveal a tangled web of consequences that demand our attention. Each strand, when pulled, can unravel the very fabric of our society, leading to unexpected problems that go far beyond the business world.

The challenges we face today require all of us to take action and be ready to adapt to a world that's always changing. It's not enough to simply watch change happen; we need to engage with it. Embracing innovation and transformation isn't just a personal journey—it's a responsibility we all share. As we witness the fallout from industries that have chosen to do nothing, it becomes clear that the cost of remaining stagnant goes well beyond the boardroom; it affects the heart of our communities and our planet.

As we navigate this complex landscape, we must prioritize not only technological advancement but also how to fairly distribute its rewards. This means investing in education and training so that the workforce is equipped with the skills needed to thrive in a changing economy. It also means pushing for policies that address inequality and create opportunities for everyone, no matter their background. Only by recognizing how our choices are connected can we hope to reduce the consequences of inaction.

As we reach this pivotal moment, it's important to remember that the choice is ours to make. We can either cling to the past, holding on to outdated practices and ideas, or we can welcome the future, stepping into a new era of innovation and progress. The decision to take action—or not—will shape not just our individual paths but the future direction of society itself. The real question is: which path will we choose? Will we learn from the stories of those who came before us, or will we repeat their mistakes? Reflecting on the lessons from Blockbuster and Kodak, let's acknowledge that, in the end, the consequences of inaction are a weight we all share.

A Call to Action

Change is in the air, and it's urgent. The days of sitting back and waiting are behind us; the world is asking for action and a shared awakening to the possibilities ahead. Technology is advancing faster than ever, giving us tools that could reshape our society. But, even with all this progress, we see a troubling trend of stagnation. Businesses are holding on to old ways of doing things, governments are slow to embrace fresh ideas, and many individuals feel stuck in fear or uncertainty. It's high time we change this story and use technology for real, meaningful progress.

Think for a moment about a future where technology isn't just about convenience but acts as a powerful force for positive change. Imagine communities thriving not just because of the latest tech gadgets but because of innovative solutions to longstanding problems. In this future, working together matters more than competing against one another, and taking risks is something to celebrate, not shy away from. Each of us has a part to play in making this vision a reality. It begins with reigniting our creative spirits and understanding that failure can lead to growth—that experimenting is a key step toward success.

Creating a culture that supports experimentation means we all need to shift our mindset. We must build spaces where ideas can grow, where creativity can flourish without fear holding it back. This isn't just a job for entrepreneurs or tech companies; it's a call to action for everyone. Schools need to change, helping students develop critical thinking and problem-solving skills that prepare them for the challenges of today's world. Businesses should make innovation a top priority, rewarding those who think outside the box.

And governments must break down the bureaucratic barriers that hold us back, paving the way for bold initiatives that can truly transform our communities.

Grassroots movements play a crucial role in this change. They remind us that real progress often starts at the local level. When community members unite around a shared vision and a determination to make a difference, amazing things can happen. We've seen this with local efforts focused on sustainability, education, and social justice that have gained momentum through the passion of dedicated individuals. By getting involved in our communities, we not only challenge complacency but also spark a ripple effect that encourages others to join in. The power of collective action is profound; movements can influence policies, reshape industries, and ultimately change societal norms.

The urgency of our current situation cannot be ignored. The consequences of inaction are staggering—our planet is in danger, economies are struggling, and inequalities are growing. But the chance for change has never been clearer. As we find ourselves at this crucial moment, we must harness the potential of technology to tackle these pressing issues. From renewable energy solutions to advancements in healthcare, the innovations available to us can help combat climate change, promote fairness, and improve lives across the board.

However, to take advantage of these opportunities, we must be ready to step outside our comfort zones. The fear of failure shouldn't keep us from moving forward—it should push us to try harder. Every setback teaches us something valuable that can set the stage for greater success if we embrace it. The road to innovation isn't always easy, but staying determined is key. Let's remember the stories of those who dared to break the mold—the visionaries, the risk-takers, the advocates for change. They show us that the journey toward progress can be tough, but it's also filled with possibilities.

In this shared effort, we must also emphasize the importance of inclusivity. Every voice counts, and every perspective enriches the conversation. By creating environments where diverse opinions and experiences are welcomed, we can deepen our understanding of the challenges we face and the solutions that can arise. This inclusiveness will help us tap into a wide range of ideas and innovations that are crucial for addressing the complex issues of our time.

As we look ahead, let's hold onto the lessons from the past. We must stay alert against the temptation of complacency and listen to those who have faced the harsh consequences of inaction. The stakes are high, but so are the rewards of taking courageous steps forward. By coming together in our pursuit of progress, we can shape a future defined by innovation, resilience, and fairness.

Now is the time to act, to raise our goals, and to embrace the amazing potential of technology. We can't afford to wait for change to happen; we need to be the change. Together, let's rise to the challenge ahead, inspired by the promise of a brighter tomorrow. The future isn't something that just happens to us—it's something we create together. So let's pick up our pens, step onto the canvas of our lives, and paint a reality that shows our greatest hopes.

Cornel Jefferson

Chapter 2: The Rise of Effective Accelerationism

Foundations of Effective Accelerationism

Throughout history, societies have swung between times of rapid growth and periods of stagnation, often driven by technological advancements that promised a brighter future. Many people today feel that we are stuck in one of those stagnant periods. A sense of inertia seems to hold us back, anchoring us to outdated practices and limiting our dreams of what the future can be. But even in this challenging landscape, a bright idea has begun to shine: Effective Accelerationism (e/acc). This transformative way of thinking sees technology as a powerful force for social progress, encouraging us to tap into its full potential. To truly grasp what e/acc is all about, we need to explore its philosophical and historical roots, uncovering the key principles that give life to this movement.

The ideas behind Effective Accelerationism can be traced back to the Enlightenment, when reason, science, and progress were celebrated as signs of human advancement. Influential thinkers like Francis

Bacon and Karl Popper pushed for the use of empirical evidence and rational thinking as paths to knowledge. Their work fostered a belief that humanity could shape its own future through innovation and critical inquiry. Bacon called for advancing knowledge through experimentation, while Popper highlighted the importance of testing scientific theories, inspiring a culture of questioning and improvement. These early concepts laid the groundwork for the idea that technological progress is not just desirable but necessary for society to evolve.

Fast forward to the late 20th century, and we see the beginnings of Effective Accelerationism taking root in the fields of cybernetics and systems theory. As we started to understand how systems interconnect and how feedback loops operate within technological ecosystems, it became clear that technology could be more than just a tool; it could be a force for transformation. The rise of computers, the internet, and artificial intelligence brought about a major shift, changing not only industries but also the way people interact with one another. The idea that technology could enhance human abilities and open up previously closed doors became a rallying cry for thinkers and innovators alike.

However, not everyone has embraced technological progress without hesitation. The 21st century has seen a growing backlash against the rapid pace of change. Critics often raise concerns about the ethical dilemmas posed by new technologies, the environmental toll of industrialization, and the increasing economic divide worsened by automation. This is where Effective Accelerationism stands out. Unlike more pessimistic views, e/acc encourages a proactive approach to technology, urging us to face its challenges directly instead of retreating into doubt or despair. This isn't about blindly trusting technology; it's about using it as a tool for the greater good.

At the core of Effective Accelerationism lies a set of principles that guide its supporters—starting with a strong commitment to innovation. e/acc promotes the belief that progress is an ongoing process, encouraging individuals and organizations to constantly seek out new ideas, question the status quo, and try out new solutions. This mindset creates an environment where creativity can thrive, redefining the fear of failure as a chance for growth. In this way, obstacles and setbacks are seen not as barriers but as stepping stones on the path to success.

Another key aspect of e/acc is the ethical responsibility that comes with technological advancement. The saying "with great power comes great responsibility" rings true within the e/acc movement. Advocates stress that embracing technology should not sacrifice social equity or environmental health. Instead, the goal is to create solutions that uplift communities, protect our planet, and ensure that everyone benefits from innovation. This ethical perspective encourages us to engage in thoughtful conversations about the consequences of our technological choices, fostering a culture where responsible action goes hand in hand with progress.

Inclusivity is another important principle that enriches the foundation of Effective Accelerationism. This movement recognizes the wide variety of ideas, voices, and perspectives that contribute to technological advancement. By promoting collaboration across different fields, regions, and backgrounds, e/acc creates a vibrant ecosystem of innovation that draws from humanity's collective wisdom. This inclusivity is more than just a nice idea; it's a necessity. The challenges we face today—such as climate change, healthcare inequality, and social injustice—demand multifaceted solutions that can only come from diverse minds working together toward a common goal.

As we think about the rise of Effective Accelerationism, it's crucial to acknowledge the historical and philosophical contexts that have shaped this ideology. We build on the work of great thinkers who recognized the power of technology and aimed to steer its course for the benefit of humanity. Their legacy reminds us that our decisions today will shape the world of tomorrow. The movement calls on us to use our technological advances with purpose and intention, crafting a shared story that values progress over stagnation.

In this quest, it becomes clear that Effective Accelerationism is not just a response to the challenges we face; it is a passionate call to action, encouraging us to unlock our potential and engage constructively with the world around us. By grounding ourselves in the core principles of innovation, ethical responsibility, and inclusivity, we can create a brighter future—one where technology acts as a bridge, connecting us to the endless possibilities that lie ahead.

The journey of Effective Accelerationism isn't just about the technology itself; it's about the people who leverage it, the values they uphold, and the social structures they aim to change. The vision of a future where technology enhances human ability and collective well-being is not just a distant dream but a tangible reality waiting to take shape. As we look at the visionaries leading the charge and the obstacles we must overcome, we will gain a deeper understanding of how Effective Accelerationism holds the key to unlocking the full potential of our diverse and dynamic society.

So, as we stand on the edge of this new era, let's hold onto our curiosity, the ethical responsibility of our choices, and the importance of inclusion as we navigate the complexities of technology and innovation. The call for Effective Accelerationism is not just a request; it's a rallying cry—encouraging us to break free from stagnation, spark our ambitions, and channel our collective creativity for a better tomorrow.

Visionaries Leading the Charge

Every transformative movement has its champions—those individuals who truly embody the principles of the ideology and push the boundaries of what we think is possible. Effective Accelerationism is no different. In the exciting world of rapid technological change, the visionaries who lead this movement are remarkable figures, each bringing unique talents and insights to the shared story of progress. Their journeys are not just inspiring; they offer us a roadmap for what can be achieved when ambition, creativity, and a sense of responsibility come together.

One of the most well-known names in the e/acc ideology is Eliezer Yudkowsky. He isn't just a theorist; he's a thought-provoking figure who challenges the status quo and urges society to face the serious challenges posed by advanced artificial intelligence. With a background in AI research and as a co-founder of the Machine Intelligence Research Institute, Yudkowsky's contributions blend both theory and practice. He highlights how crucial it is to make sure that the development of superintelligent AI aligns with human values— a huge task, for sure. His call for strict safety measures in AI development comes from a deep belief that the future of humanity relies on our ability to guide these powerful technologies responsibly.

Yudkowsky often discusses his views in ways that go beyond technical details, diving into the ethical issues surrounding AI. He warns us that if we ignore these concerns, we could end up facing disastrous outcomes. His work encourages us to ponder deep questions like: How do we define what's "good" when we have technologies that can change reality? This quest for clarity in moral philosophy resonates with the core values of Effective Accelerationism, which stress the importance of ethical responsibility alongside innovation.

Another shining star of the e/acc movement is Vitalik Buterin, the co-founder of Ethereum, a decentralized platform that has completely changed how we view finance, governance, and trust. Buterin sees more in his work than just cryptocurrency; he imagines a future where decentralized systems empower individuals, breaking down the barriers set by traditional institutions. His strong commitment to principles like transparency and democratization shines through in his work, which aims to create a more inclusive digital economy.

Buterin believes that technology should support humanity rather than control it. He embodies the spirit of Effective

Accelerationism through his efforts to promote decentralized governance, helping people take charge of their financial futures. In a time when trust in centralized authorities is dwindling, Buterin's vision gives us hope for a future where individuals have more control over their lives. The Ethereum blockchain stands as proof of this vision, creating a space for innovation that encourages teamwork and creativity.

Then there's Elon Musk, an entrepreneur whose relentless drive for progress has made him one of the most talked-about figures today. Musk captures the essence of Effective Accelerationism, actively seeking to use technology to tackle some of humanity's biggest challenges. From SpaceX's goal to colonize Mars to Tesla's mission to transform the automotive world with electric cars, Musk's projects reflect a passionate desire to go beyond the ordinary. He truly believes that technological progress is the key to overcoming challenges that feel impossible.

Musk's initiatives often spark both admiration and debate, yet they encourage broader conversations about our future. His bold ambitions make us think about our limits: Why shouldn't we aim for a future where humans can live on other planets? Why shouldn't we seek sustainable energy solutions that drastically cut down our carbon emissions? These questions inspire a shared vision of accelerationism that goes beyond individual efforts. Musk invites us to dream big and to act courageously, reminding us that the stakes have never been higher.

The tales of these visionaries highlight the variety of thoughts and actions within the Effective Accelerationism movement. They reflect different motivations that drive people to pursue technological advancement. For Yudkowsky, it's about ensuring humanity's survival in the age of advanced AI. For Buterin, it's about breaking down power structures and building fair systems. For Musk, it's about challenging the limits of human capability and tackling the existential threats we face. Each of these leaders, in their unique ways, embodies the spirit of effective accelerationism, showing how varied perspectives can unite around a common goal: using technology for the greater good.

Their stories are not just about individuals; they serve as a rallying cry for action. Effective Accelerationism asks us to embrace technology's potential and engage with the challenges it presents. These visionaries demonstrate that the future isn't a distant idea; it's a reality we can shape through our choices and actions. They invite us to envision a world where technology acts not just as an extension of ourselves, but as a partner in our pursuit of progress.

As we look at the tangible impacts these individuals have made, we see a wealth of initiatives and projects that reflect their innovative ways of tackling complex problems. For instance, Musk's push for sustainable energy through Tesla's electric vehicles and solar products offers a glimpse of a future free from fossil fuels, inspiring those who dream of a more sustainable world. The growing popularity of electric vehicles not only cuts greenhouse gas emissions but also sparks a cultural shift toward healthier living. Musk's initiatives show how one person's drive can create a ripple effect in society, encouraging others to join the fight for a cleaner planet.

Similarly, Buterin's Ethereum is more than just a financial platform; it has sparked an entire ecosystem of decentralized applications, enabling people to invent creative solutions for societal challenges. From decentralized finance (DeFi) to non-fungible tokens (NFTs), Ethereum highlights the potential of blockchain technology to empower individuals and inspire creativity. By creating a space for collaboration and innovation, Buterin has ignited a movement that encourages participation from those who may have felt left out by traditional systems.

Yudkowsky's work goes beyond mere theory; he is actively shaping the future of artificial intelligence at the Machine Intelligence Research Institute. His commitment to ensuring AI development is in line with human values is crucial as technology evolves quickly. Yudkowsky's push for safety protocols and careful testing emphasizes that ethics must be part of our journey in innovation. His contributions remind us that progress requires careful navigation, ensuring that technology improves, not endangers, our well-being.

These visionaries are just a few of the many who are driving the movement of Effective Accelerationism. Across various fields, from healthcare to environmental science, a new generation of innovators is rising, motivated by a shared desire to use technology for the good of society. Their stories illustrate the power of individual action and the incredible impact one person's vision can have on the world.

In healthcare, for example, telemedicine has changed how patients receive care. Innovators in this field are using technology to break down barriers, allowing people in remote areas to consult with healthcare professionals easily. This shift not only improves access to care but also tackles the pressing issue of healthcare inequality. By leveraging technology for better health outcomes, these pioneers reflect the principles of Effective Accelerationism, showing how tech can help create a fairer society.

Moreover, advancements in renewable energy technologies have led to a new wave of entrepreneurs dedicated to fighting climate change. From solar panel innovations to wind energy solutions, these visionaries are making strides in their fields, proving that sustainable technologies can be both profitable and beneficial for the environment. Their work serves as a powerful call for collective action, inspiring others to join the movement toward a greener future.

The stories of these visionaries remind us of the incredible power of individual action in driving collective progress. They encourage us to think about our potential to make a difference in the world. Effective Accelerationism is not just about a few brilliant minds; it's about the collective ambition of many who seek to use technology for a better society. Each story is like a spark, igniting a sense of possibility and urging us to explore how we can also contribute to this unfolding journey of progress.

As we think about what lies ahead, it becomes clear that the path of Effective Accelerationism is a shared effort, welcoming diverse voices and perspectives into the conversation. The challenges we face are not too great to handle; they are opportunities for teamwork, creativity, and innovation. By embracing inclusivity, we can create a vibrant environment where ideas thrive, and groundbreaking solutions come to life.

In the end, the visionaries leading the charge in Effective Accelerationism give us a glimpse of what can happen when we use technology with intention and purpose. Their stories inspire us to break free from stagnation, to dream without limits, and to engage with the complexities of our world. As we stand at the crossroads of technology and humanity, let's carry forward the flame of innovation, guided by the values of ethical responsibility and inclusivity. Together, we can write the next chapter in our shared story—a tale that celebrates progress, nurtures collaboration, and empowers individuals to shape a brighter future for everyone.

Breaking Barriers: Distinguishing Effective Accelerationism from Other Ideologies

In a time when discussions about technology swing between fears of a dark future and dreams of a bright one, it's easy to get lost in the confusion about what Effective Accelerationism really means. Often shortened to e/acc, Effective Accelerationism offers a fresh outlook focused on using technology to improve society while steering clear of both extreme optimism and pessimistic retreat. Grasping its subtleties is crucial, not just for those involved in the movement, but also for anyone eager to connect meaningfully with the world around them.

At its heart, Effective Accelerationism is all about intention. It's not just about jumping on the technology bandwagon for the sake of progress; it's about applying technology thoughtfully to achieve specific goals. Many people mistakenly think e/acc is simply about speeding up technological trends without caring about where they lead. This view is completely opposite to what the movement stands for, which is that technology's growth should come with a strong set of ethical guidelines. Effective Accelerationism emphasizes that with great power comes great responsibility, urging its supporters to prioritize the careful and thoughtful use of technology in ways that truly benefit people and improve society.

So how does this differ from other ideologies that seem to share similar themes? For example, consider the technophilia often seen in Silicon Valley, where there's a tendency to idolize technology as a one-size-fits-all solution for humanity's challenges. This point of view often overlooks the inherent risks and treats any negatives as mere bumps in the road rather than serious concerns that deserve attention. In contrast, e/acc recognizes the potential downsides of quick technological advancements and actively works to address these challenges through careful thinking and planning. The movement calls for a responsible approach to innovation, one that strives to foresee the impacts of technology on our daily lives.

Moreover, it's vital to differentiate Effective Accelerationism from more pessimistic stories that spread a sense of hopelessness about technological progress. These fear-driven narratives tend to spotlight only the negative effects of rapid advancements, like job losses due to automation or the risks posed by artificial intelligence. While these worries are legitimate and deserve our attention, they can create a mindset that stifles productive conversations about solutions. Advocates of e/acc recognize that while staying vigilant is important, it's equally crucial to take proactive steps to influence the direction of technology in ways that uplift our values and dreams.

The difference between Effective Accelerationism and fear-based narratives can be likened to the distinction between a ship caught in a storm and one that navigates through it. The former gets tossed around by the waves, while the latter uses the wind to reach its destination. e/acc doesn't shy away from acknowledging the challenges that come with rapid technological change; instead, it focuses on steering our course with intention and purpose.

Furthermore, the overly optimistic visions presented by some in the transhumanist movement can often blur the lines of Effective Accelerationism. These inspiring dreams may depict a future where technology magically solves all of humanity's problems, but they often fail to address the complex socio-political realities we face. This kind of uncritical optimism can lead to overlooking the ethical implications of technological growth, which could widen the gap between what technology can offer and the actual experiences of people.

In contrast, Effective Accelerationism takes a practical route that celebrates technological potential while remaining grounded in the social realities of today. It fosters a vision of the future that's both compelling and realistic, recognizing existing inequalities and suggesting ways to overcome them. e/acc seeks to understand how technology can help empower marginalized communities rather than worsen current disparities. This blend of optimism and practicality is what makes e/acc stand out compared to overly idealistic or negative viewpoints.

A significant part of this exploration involves identifying the ideological barriers that hold back progress. As technology advances, societies often cling to familiar ways of thinking and resist change out of fear. This kind of fear-based resistance can create an atmosphere where innovation is met with suspicion instead of curiosity. Effective Accelerationism aims to break down these barriers by promoting a culture that values experimentation and learning, even—and especially—when failure is a possibility.

  Supporters of e/acc stress the need to create environments where ideas can grow without the constraints of outdated traditions. This isn't just about technological innovation; it's also about social innovation. The movement challenges the belief that change must always be disruptive and chaotic. Instead, it argues that change can happen naturally through teamwork, shared knowledge, and a willingness to adapt. By doing this, e/acc encourages societies to rethink their relationship with technology, viewing it not as a threat but as a partner in progress.

  Looking at Effective Accelerationism alongside other ideologies reveals key differences in mindset, goals, and methods. While some movements might suggest that technological solutions should be imposed from above, e/acc champions grassroots involvement and making technology accessible to everyone. It advocates for the idea that those impacted by technological changes should have a voice in the decision-making process. This inclusive approach fosters a sense of shared responsibility and accountability, which is crucial for building trust in the technological developments that shape our lives.

The objectives of Effective Accelerationism are also distinct. While other ideologies might focus solely on technology as an end goal, e/acc sees technology as a means to reach broader societal aims like justice, equity, and sustainability. The movement encourages a reevaluation of what success looks like, pushing stakeholders to consider not just how fast technology is advancing but also how it affects people's well-being and the health of our planet. This comprehensive outlook drives e/acc advocates to explore how technology can address urgent global issues, from climate change to health crises, in ways that are both innovative and responsible.

When it comes to methods, Effective Accelerationism actively promotes collaboration across various fields, drawing insights from sociology, ethics, engineering, and environmental science. This integrative approach allows for a deeper understanding of the complexities involved in blending technology into our lives, ensuring that a range of perspectives is part of the conversation. By encouraging dialogue across disciplines, e/acc creates a rich atmosphere where ideas can mix and lead to groundbreaking innovations informed by multiple viewpoints.

The conversation around Effective Accelerationism calls for a change in how we think about technology in our societies. It prompts us to think about our shared responsibilities as innovators, consumers, and leaders. Effective Accelerationism isn't just a response to technological change; it's a proactive approach that aims to guide that change toward positive outcomes for everyone. By breaking down the barriers and misunderstandings, we can start to recognize the transformative potential of a movement that puts ethical responsibility and purpose at the forefront of our technological endeavors.

Looking at it this way, it's clear that Effective Accelerationism is positioned at a pivotal point in the ongoing conversation about technology and society. It provides a framework for navigating the challenges of our modern world, encouraging us to embrace both the good and the bad that come with swift technological growth. By advocating for a shared approach rooted in ethical values and open dialogue, e/acc paves the way for a future that not only speeds up progress but does so in a way that uplifts and empowers everyone.

As we consider these differences, it's clear that the vision of Effective Accelerationism is not just about the future of technology; it's about the future of humanity itself. It urges us to rethink our relationship with the tools we create, guiding us to innovate with a sense of purpose that aligns with our shared values and dreams. In doing so, Effective Accelerationism opens a pathway toward a fairer, more just, and sustainable world, where technology acts as a force for human flourishing rather than a source of division.

Through this perspective, we can see that the road ahead is full of promise. The challenges we face are significant, but they also present chances for resilience and creativity. By nurturing a culture of collaboration and ethical responsibility, effective accelerationists are not just navigating through rough waters; they are plotting a course towards uncharted territories of opportunity, all while making sure that the journey reflects the diverse experiences that define the human condition.

The story of Effective Accelerationism is one of hope—a recognition that, even if the future is uncertain, it's also filled with possibilities for those willing to engage with the complexities of technology in a thoughtful and intentional way. As we find ourselves at this crucial moment in our technological journey, let's take on the responsibilities that come with it, working together to harness the power of innovation for the common good. The call to action is clear: we must dismantle the barriers that hold us back from a brighter future and come together in our quest for a world where technology shines as a beacon of opportunity for all.

Cornel Jefferson

Chapter 3: The Fallacy of Degrowth

Understanding the Degrowth Movement

The Degrowth Movement has become more popular over the last few decades. Its main idea is that constantly chasing economic growth isn't just impractical, but it can also hurt the environment and lead to unfairness in society. Supporters of degrowth imagine a world where living well is more important than consuming more and more stuff. This brings up big questions about what we value and what we really want in life. At its heart, the movement pushes back against rampant consumerism and the environmental damage that often comes with traditional growth models. Instead, it promotes simpler living, moderation, and a shift toward local economies.

People who support degrowth believe that our current path of endless economic growth is damaging. It not only leads to the exhaustion of our natural resources but also makes social inequalities worse. They argue that we should rethink what it means to live a good life, suggesting that real happiness can come from focusing on sustainability, community, and a deeper connection with our surroundings. This view is often influenced by various philosophies, like eco-socialism and anarchism, which highlight the importance of living together and taking care of our environment.

However, while the arguments for degrowth might resonate with those worried about the planet and the growing gaps between the rich and the poor, there are some serious flaws in this way of thinking that we should look closely at. First, the idea that limiting growth can truly solve environmental problems is tricky and doesn't have a lot of real-world proof to back it up. History shows that economic downturns can lead to increased poverty, job loss, and social unrest, which can undermine the fairness that degrowth advocates want to achieve. If we genuinely want to build a fairer society, we should shift our focus from limiting growth to making sure that the benefits of new technology and innovation are shared fairly among everyone.

Additionally, the call to simplify our lives and cut back on consumption, while it sounds appealing, raises practical questions about how it could affect human creativity and potential. Many of humanity's greatest achievements—like medical breakthroughs, technological advancements, and brilliant works of art—have come during times of growth and exploration. Promoting a degrowth mentality might unintentionally limit the creativity and ambition that have driven us forward. Our natural instinct is to innovate, dream big, and push boundaries. Asking people to give up these dreams for the sake of sustainability could not only backfire but also let down future generations who will need our creativity to tackle their challenges.

When we take a closer look at the ideas behind the Degrowth Movement, it's essential to question the broader effects of adopting such a limiting perspective. Advocates for degrowth often take a moral stance, suggesting that consumption is harmful. This viewpoint can overlook the many ways people contribute to their communities and the global economy. Saying that we all need to consume less to save the planet might sound good in theory, but it simplifies the complex relationship between what we buy and its impact on the environment.

To illustrate, let's think about renewable energy. Technologies like solar panels, wind turbines, and electric vehicles are significant steps toward producing energy in a more sustainable way. However, these innovations require resources, investment, and growth—things that supporters of degrowth might dismiss as contrary to their beliefs. The contradiction here is that growth can happen within the context of sustainable technologies without repeating the harmful practices of the past. Instead, this new kind of growth can respect ecological principles and help create a balanced relationship between people and our planet.

Moreover, while it's true that we must not continue to use up our natural resources at the current pace, this view ignores the exciting potential of new technologies to change how we interact with those resources. Innovations like carbon capture, alternative proteins, and better waste management systems can help us minimize the negative effects of consumption. These technologies can help us achieve a balance that respects our ecological limits while still allowing for growth. If we only focus on reducing consumption, we might overlook these groundbreaking solutions that could lead us to a brighter and more sustainable future.

While supporters of degrowth envision a simpler world, we must face the realities of human ambition and the complexities of modern life. Suggesting that we can or should go back to a more basic way of living overlooks our natural desire to create, explore, and improve our lives. Throughout history, times of stagnation have often led to despair, conflict, and setbacks. The idea that we can simply halt progress and expect a perfect world to magically appear is unrealistic and overlooks the complexities of human nature and society.

As we look into the implications of the Degrowth Movement, it becomes clear that a more effective approach would be to encourage innovation and welcome new technologies as tools for positive change. Instead of retreating into a mindset of scarcity, we should focus our collective energy on redefining what growth means in today's world. This means embracing the possibility of sustainable development that goes beyond just economic measures and prioritizes well-being, fairness, and caring for the environment.

To redefine growth, we first need to accept that it's not inherently bad. Often portrayed as the villain in our ecological story, growth can actually be a force for good when it aligns with sustainable practices and fair distribution. The challenge isn't to reject growth altogether; it's to reshape our understanding of it so that it benefits everyone.

One of the strongest arguments against degrowth is its possible impact on human potential and the future of our societies. Painting growth as a villain could discourage people from pursuing their dreams, which are often what drive them to seek a better life. The stories of human progress are full of individuals who, fueled by ambition and creativity, have worked to improve their lives and the world around them. It's vital that we empower these dreamers instead of limiting their aspirations in the name of sustainability.

Moreover, we must not overlook the intertwined nature of today's global economy. The world we live in is a vast web of connections—bound by trade, culture, and shared challenges. Adopting a degrowth mindset could cut these connections, leading to isolation and worsening inequalities, making it harder to tackle global issues like climate change, poverty, and health crises. A bright future requires us to embrace a vision of progress that is inclusive, innovative, and expansive—one that acknowledges our shared humanity and interconnected fates.

As we dig deeper into the foundations of the Degrowth Movement, we should also consider the alternative ideas that push back against its claims. There is a vision of a world where growth and sustainability can work together in harmony. This invites us to explore new economic models, like circular economies, which focus on using resources wisely and cutting down waste while still allowing for growth. By nurturing a culture of innovation and inspiring individuals and organizations to think creatively about their roles in creating a more sustainable future, we can rise above the limits set by the degrowth viewpoint.

The conversations around economic growth, sustainability, and social fairness are intricate and multifaceted, too complex to be narrowed down to simple slogans or opposing sides. They require thoughtful dialogue, a readiness to question our beliefs, and the bravery to imagine a future that makes the most of human potential. Instead of falling back into a mindset of scarcity, we should challenge ourselves to rethink what is possible when we combine technology, creativity, and human ambition for the benefit of everyone.

Ultimately, it's not about choosing between growth or degrowth; it's about fostering a mindset that harnesses the best of both. By breaking free from the constraints of rigid ideologies, we can open the door to a new era of prosperity that enhances human potential, encourages innovation, and honors the delicate balance of our environment. It's time to leave behind the dogmas that hold us back and embrace the endless possibilities ahead of us. In doing so, we can equip ourselves with the tools needed to navigate the complexities of our world and build a future that is both sustainable and rich with opportunity.

Limiting Human Potential

The idea of degrowth comes from a good place, focusing on sustainability and the environment. However, it often sends an underlying message: to create a better world, we need to hold ourselves back. While this idea is well-intentioned, it creates a tricky situation that we need to think about more deeply. In our search for a sustainable future, the degrowth philosophy could actually suppress our human potential and stifle the creativity, innovation, and entrepreneurial spirit that have historically helped us improve our lives and advance society.

Let's take a look at the technology sector, which has drastically changed our lives and economies. Many technological breakthroughs have happened during times of growth, driven by our desire to solve important problems. For example, consider the internet. It was created to connect people and share information, leading to amazing communication, teamwork, and economic growth. But if we adopt a degrowth mindset, we might end up choking off the very innovations that empower individuals and communities.

Innovation flourishes when we explore, take risks, and feel free to try new things—qualities that often clash with a mindset focused on limitations. Seeing economic growth as a bad thing may create an atmosphere where people shy away from chasing their dreams, worried that their ambitions might lead to unsustainable practices. This fear could lead to stagnation, leaving us unprepared to face the many challenges ahead.

To highlight this, let's look at a few examples of companies and nations that have embraced growth and innovation, finding success while also addressing environmental concerns. Take Tesla, for instance. It has become a leader in electric vehicles not just by promoting less consumption but by rethinking the future of transportation. Through its dedication to sustainability, Tesla demonstrates that economic growth can go hand in hand with tackling climate change. Rather than retreating into a mindset of scarcity, Tesla's vision pushes us toward a future where technology helps solve environmental issues.

Similarly, countries like Denmark have become frontrunners in renewable energy by investing in clean technologies. Thanks to its strong focus on wind energy, Denmark has transformed itself into a global leader in sustainable practices, all while fostering economic growth and creating jobs. By championing innovation and technological progress, Denmark has improved its living standards and environmental performance, providing a powerful counter-example to the degrowth idea.

The contradictions of degrowth really stand out when we think about the possible fallout from limiting human potential. The creativity that propels progress and solutions often thrives on economic opportunity. When people feel encouraged to take risks, pursue their passions, and think outside the box, they can come up with groundbreaking ideas to address the pressing issues we face. This dynamic between ambition and opportunity has driven humanity forward, helping us tackle complex problems like disease, poverty, and environmental degradation.

On the flip side, promoting degrowth might unintentionally lead to a culture of complacency. While the idea of simplifying our lives and consuming less can be tempting, it may also dampen the ambition that has historically led to real change. The notion that we should settle for less could stifle the drive for improvement that has shaped our societies. By putting limits on human potential, we risk turning away the very individuals who could lead us toward a more sustainable future.

Adding another layer to this discussion is the interconnectedness of our global economy. In a world where trade, collaboration, and shared knowledge fuel our progress, adopting a degrowth mindset could cause isolation and worsen existing inequalities. Focusing on limiting consumption might hamper international partnerships, making it harder for us to tackle global challenges like climate change and health crises together.

We can see the remarkable benefits of international collaboration through initiatives like the development of vaccines during the COVID-19 pandemic. Countries, scientists, and pharmaceutical companies came together to share knowledge and resources, leading to the rapid creation and distribution of vaccines that have saved countless lives. This achievement didn't arise from a mindset of limitation; it was driven by the desire to innovate and improve lives through teamwork and growth.

If we really want to face the pressing issues of our time, we should embrace a vision that sees growth as a way to create positive change. There's a wealth of potential for innovation in every corner of our society, just waiting to be tapped into. The challenge isn't in rejecting growth, but in redefining what it means in terms of sustainability and social equity. We need to foster a mindset where innovation is viewed as a key tool for addressing the ecological and social challenges we face, rather than as something to be feared.

One way to rethink growth is through the idea of a circular economy. This model highlights sustainability by encouraging the reuse, repair, and recycling of materials to reduce waste. By adopting circular economy principles, we can leverage growth to build systems that are environmentally friendly while also driving economic development. This approach aligns with sustainable values while empowering individuals and businesses to innovate.

Additionally, we should remember that some of the biggest advancements in human history have occurred during periods of growth. For instance, progress in medicine and public health has consistently been linked to economic expansion. The quest for innovation in healthcare not only boosts individual health but also strengthens society as a whole. Limiting growth could jeopardize our ability to keep advancing in these essential areas.

Let's not underestimate the power of human ambition and creativity. Throughout history, people have stepped up to solve seemingly impossible challenges. The story of humanity is one of relentless pursuit—of knowledge, progress, and improvement. We need to create an environment where this spirit thrives, encouraging everyone to dream big and break barriers.

At its heart, the case against degrowth isn't denying the need for sustainability or social equity. Instead, it's about understanding that we can achieve these goals through growth, innovation, and collaboration. We need to shift our focus from limiting and reducing to recognizing the potential for positive change that harnesses our human creativity. By promoting a broad vision of progress, we can pave the way for a more fair and sustainable future.

As we consider the implications of restricting human potential, it's clear we need to create a space that encourages exploration and innovation. We are living in a critical moment—one that asks us to use all we've learned to challenge complacency and inspire meaningful change. The world is filled with opportunities, and by redefining growth to prioritize sustainability and social equity, we can craft a future that not only meets today's needs but also empowers generations to come.

We are on the edge of a new era defined by innovation, collaboration, and creativity. By welcoming growth into our discussions, we can unlock the immense potential of human ingenuity to reshape our world for the better. This isn't a call to abandon our commitment to sustainability; rather, it's an invitation to rethink what's possible when we harness the power of innovation for the greater good. By doing so, we can build a future where human potential flourishes, creativity knows no limits, and the pursuit of progress goes hand in hand with caring for our planet and ensuring social equity.

Rejecting Constraints

In a world that often feels full of limits—both those we place on ourselves and those imposed by outside forces—the spirit of innovation can seem under siege. The common story, driven by worries about sustainability and the scarcity of resources, has led many people to adopt a mindset that focuses on cutting back instead of expanding. This way of thinking, rooted in the degrowth movement, creates an atmosphere where reduction is seen as a virtue. But what if we turned that idea upside down? What if, rather than retreating into a shell of limitations, we boldly embraced a vision of Effective Accelerationism, where our shared goal is not just to survive but to truly thrive?

This isn't just a change in thinking; it's a powerful call to action. Embracing a mindset of growth means recognizing the incredible well of human creativity and technological potential we all have. It invites us to see that the challenges we face today—whether it's climate change, social inequality, or economic instability—aren't impossible obstacles, but rather chances for innovation. When we refuse to be held back by constraints, we spark the flame of possibility, turning challenges into stepping stones for progress.

Our future depends on how well we can nurture a culture that values innovation, teamwork, and the courage to dream big. Individuals, businesses, and governments all have a role to play in this transformation. It starts with policies that support research and development, offering incentives for companies that dare to think big and venture into new areas. Picture a world where every business isn't just a participant in the economy, but a trailblazer, driven by the quest for groundbreaking solutions. This can become a reality when we shift our focus from fearing excess to celebrating ingenuity.

On top of that, we can't overlook the importance of clean technologies. As we face the challenges of caring for our environment, the conversation about growth needs to change. Investing in renewable energy sources—like solar and wind—shouldn't be seen as a sacrifice but as a chance to raise our living standards while protecting our planet. Instead of a story of giving things up, we can tell a story of mutual growth, where economic progress and environmental responsibility go hand in hand.

Entrepreneurship is vital to this vision. The entrepreneurial spirit thrives on taking risks, being creative, and tirelessly seeking solutions. When we cultivate an environment that supports startups and innovative thinkers, we foster a fertile ground for new ideas to take root. Governments can play a crucial role by simplifying regulations and offering financial support to budding companies. When young innovators are empowered, they become heroes of change, pushing forward the technologies that will shape our future.

But it's not just about businesses and governments; we all need to adopt this mindset. Each of us has the ability to contribute to a culture of innovation. We should build resilience and adaptability, seeing obstacles not as roadblocks but as chances to be inventive. This way of thinking can change our everyday experiences—from how we approach our work to our interactions in our communities. Imagine a neighborhood that bands together to tackle local issues with creativity and teamwork. This is what rejecting constraints looks like: a mindset that welcomes challenges and uses them to improve our lives together.

Take a look at how the world came together during the COVID-19 pandemic. In a time of crisis, scientists and researchers from around the globe collaborated like never before. They shared resources, exchanged knowledge, and worked tirelessly to develop vaccines at lightning speed. This wasn't a moment defined by fear or limitations; it showed us just how powerful human creativity can be. This experience should inspire us to keep that momentum alive beyond times of crisis. The same spirit that drove scientists to innovate can—and should—be applied across all sectors—healthcare, education, technology, and more.

Innovation isn't just a trendy term; it's a lifeline. When we channel our energies into creativity and exploration, we open ourselves up to opportunities we once thought were impossible. As we work toward a sustainable and fair future, we need to understand that the answers to our biggest challenges won't come from retreating into limits, but from a bold commitment to broaden our horizons.

The path to a future shaped by innovation requires us to rethink what growth truly means. It's not about mindless expansion or reckless consumption; it's about redefining growth to match the principles of sustainability and social responsibility. This new perspective allows us to imagine a world where economic development is directly tied to improving our lives and taking care of our planet. It's a world where we don't just aim to lessen our impact but to enhance our contributions.

A powerful change awaits us if we can all shift our perspectives together. Imagine cities that prosper not just from economic success but from social well-being and environmental health. Urban areas could become vibrant hubs of innovation, where clean energy solutions, green spaces, and sustainable transportation come together to improve the quality of life for everyone. In this kind of setting, technology and nature can coexist harmoniously, building a sense of community while addressing the urgent need for climate action.

In the business world, companies can adopt a threefold focus—putting equal importance on people, the planet, and profits. This isn't just a passing trend; it's a movement recognizing that long-term success comes from creating value beyond just financial gain. By concentrating on holistic growth, businesses can become agents of change, launching initiatives that benefit society while still meeting their goals.

Moreover, embracing a culture of innovation means breaking away from traditional ways of thinking. It requires us to be open to exploring unconventional solutions and questioning the status quo. In doing so, we must create an environment that rewards experimentation, celebrating both successes and failures as valuable learning experiences. A society that encourages risk-taking nurtures a relentless search for improvement, where new ideas can thrive free from the constraints of outdated beliefs.

Collaboration is key. No single organization holds all the answers; it's through teamwork—between businesses, governments, educational institutions, and individuals—that we will discover new possibilities. Partnerships can lead to impactful solutions, tapping into diverse viewpoints and expertise. These collaborations can come in many forms, from public-private partnerships that build essential infrastructure to grassroots movements that advocate for social change. The goal is to build a system where all stakeholders work together, driven by a common vision of progress.

As we picture a future where technology and human creativity work hand in hand, we can't forget how important education is in this change. An educational system that promotes critical thinking, creativity, and problem-solving skills will prepare future generations to tackle the challenges ahead. By prioritizing a curriculum that emphasizes innovation and adaptability, we can cultivate a populace ready to face adversity and inspired to create solutions.

 At the core of this vision lies a deep sense of optimism. The belief that we can overcome challenges through innovation and teamwork isn't just hopeful thinking; it's a necessary mindset for navigating our complex world. When we reject the limitations set by outdated ideas, we reaffirm our commitment to a future where human potential is fully realized. It is a future where we celebrate ambition, creativity, and a shared duty to support one another.

 In this quest for growth and innovation, we must stay true to the values of fairness and inclusivity. As we open ourselves up to the possibilities of expansion, we should make sure that the benefits of progress reach everyone. This means actively working to break down barriers and ensuring that marginalized voices are heard and empowered. By fostering a culture that embraces diversity and inclusivity, we enhance our collective problem-solving abilities, making sure a wide range of perspectives are included.

Ultimately, the journey toward rejecting constraints in favor of innovation and growth requires courage and determination. It calls on each of us to step outside our comfort zones, challenge existing narratives, and advocate for a future that reflects our highest hopes. The world is brimming with potential just waiting to be tapped into through our combined efforts.

As we come together in pursuit of a brighter future, let's remain steadfast in our commitment to progress. We must champion a vision that values innovation, collaboration, and the tireless pursuit of solutions. The time has come to cast aside the constraints that have held us back for too long and embrace the endless possibilities that lie ahead. Together, we can create a world where technology and human creativity unite to build a prosperous and fair future for all.

Chapter 4: Unleashing Technological Titans

Artificial Intelligence Revolution

The rise of Artificial Intelligence (AI) is a groundbreaking moment in our history. It's not just about machines following commands; it's about changing how we live our everyday lives. Picture this: a car that knows the best route for you, a home that adjusts itself to your needs without you having to do a thing, and a healthcare system that tailors treatment plans based on your unique genetic makeup. This isn't something from a sci-fi movie; it's the world we're stepping into quickly. The path to this future filled with AI is exciting but also comes with its fair share of challenges. To truly understand where we're headed, we need to explore these aspects more closely.

A common misunderstanding about AI is that it's just an advanced gadget that can do tasks really well. Sure, AI can help with things like organizing deliveries, improving customer service, and sifting through huge piles of data faster than we ever could. But thinking of AI as just another tech tool doesn't do justice to its incredible potential. AI is opening up new possibilities for how we can use data—not just to make existing processes better, but to create entirely new ways of thinking and acting. It's the driving force behind innovation, helping entire industries move forward in ways we can't yet fully grasp.

Take a look at the healthcare field, for instance. AI is not just about making scheduling easier or keeping track of patient files; it's helping scientists and doctors make major breakthroughs in how we diagnose and treat illnesses. Machine learning algorithms can analyze thousands of medical images in the blink of an eye, spotting patterns that even the most experienced doctors might miss. This ability leads to quicker and more accurate diagnoses of conditions like cancer. While this shows just a glimpse of what AI can do, it also raises important questions about ethics, trust, and responsibility. As we let AI take on bigger roles in decision-making, we need to think carefully about what that means for us.

Of course, not everyone is on board with AI. Many people raise valid concerns about privacy, job loss, and biases in algorithm decisions. These worries are real and deserve our attention. The key challenge isn't to stop progress; it's to guide it in a responsible and inclusive way. We must create rules and frameworks that ensure AI is used ethically, with fairness and transparency built right in. The discussions we have now about AI's role in society will set the stage for its future for years to come.

One of the most exciting parts of the AI revolution is how it can level the playing field. In the past, access to powerful technologies was often reserved for those with lots of money or expertise. Now, with more AI tools available, smaller businesses and individuals can tap into capabilities that used to belong only to huge corporations. Startups are using AI to shake things up in traditional industries, coming up with new solutions that meet consumer needs in fresh ways. With the right support, this trend could spark a wave of creativity and entrepreneurship like we've never seen before.

However, as we welcome this broader access to AI, we must also think about its impact on jobs. What about the millions of workers whose jobs might disappear because of automation? It's crucial that we start talking about how to retrain and upskill the workforce, so people are ready for the jobs of the future. Our education systems need to evolve to make sure the next generation has the skills to thrive in a world dominated by AI. Skills like critical thinking, creativity, and emotional intelligence—areas where humans shine—will be more valuable than ever as machines take on more routine tasks.

This AI revolution is more than just a tech shift; it's a wake-up call for lawmakers, educators, and business leaders to rethink their strategies and priorities. We're on the edge of a new era where humans and machines collaborate. The most successful organizations will be those that know how to blend the strengths of both. This partnership requires us to change how we see technology—from viewing it as a threat to embracing it as a helpful ally.

The role of government in this change is incredibly important. Regulations need to keep up with new technology, encouraging innovation while also protecting the public. This balance is tricky, and the stakes are high. If regulations are too strict, they could choke off innovation and drive talent away. On the flip side, if there are no rules at all, we could see abuses of power and deepen existing inequalities. Finding the right balance isn't just a policy issue; it's a moral duty that needs input from a wide range of voices, including technologists, ethicists, and people from all walks of life.

AI is constantly changing, and as technology grows, so does our understanding of its impact. Researchers and developers are always working to improve algorithms and discover new uses. This relentless push for innovation is a hallmark of the tech industry and highlights the need for flexible policies that can adapt to new developments. The days of rigid regulations are behind us; we need to create an environment that encourages experimentation and quick adjustments.

Moreover, the global nature of the AI revolution means we need to work together across borders. Countries are racing to be leaders in AI research and development, but this competition should also come with a spirit of collaboration. Sharing knowledge, best practices, and ethical guidelines is key to making sure AI is a force for good around the world instead of creating divisions. The complexities of AI require us to look beyond our national interests and work towards a shared vision for the future.

As we navigate this exciting new territory, it's crucial to keep the conversation open to all viewpoints. We should welcome input from academics, industry leaders, ethicists, and everyday people alike, all coming together with a common goal: to unlock the amazing potential of AI for the benefit of humanity. This means creating space for differing opinions and nurturing an environment where deep discussions can flourish. The future isn't set in stone; it's shaped by our decisions, our advocacy, and our commitment to building a fair and just society.

In this age of AI, we need to take on the role of responsible caretakers of technology. The choices we make today about developing, using, and regulating AI will echo through history. We have the chance—and the duty—to ensure that AI serves not just for profit but as a powerful force for positive change. This isn't just a mission for those in tech; it's a call for all of us to get involved in crafting the story of AI and where it fits into our world.

As we stand at this crossroads of opportunity and responsibility, let's remember that true progress is measured not by the power of our algorithms, but by the positive impact we create for people and communities. The AI revolution is here, and how we decide to engage with it will shape the future for generations. It's a journey filled with both promise and challenges, but if we approach it with open minds and caring hearts, we can build a future that not only utilizes technology but also lifts humanity. The road ahead may be tough, but with shared vision and intentional action, we can make sure that the AI revolution serves as a force for good, guiding society toward a brighter future.

Beyond Boundaries

The world stands at the brink of a technological transformation that could change our lives in ways we can't even begin to imagine. While artificial intelligence grabs headlines with its rapid growth, we must remember that AI doesn't operate alone. It's just one piece of a larger puzzle, woven together with exciting advancements in fields like biotechnology, quantum computing, and renewable energy. Together, these innovations are setting the stage for a smarter and more sustainable future.

Picture a world where climate change isn't a looming threat but a challenge we can conquer. Biotechnology is leading the way, transforming agriculture with genetically modified organisms (GMOs) designed to thrive despite the harsh realities of climate change. These breakthroughs promise food security for our growing population. Farmers won't just be at the mercy of unpredictable weather; they'll have tools to grow crops that withstand tough conditions. This means countries can rely less on imports and become more self-sufficient when it comes to food production. The potential is not just vast; it's thrilling!

Think about how these advancements could impact everyday lives. A small farmer in a rural community could harness biotechnology to boost crop yields even during droughts. This not only enhances their livelihood but also strengthens the local economy and builds community resilience. As biotechnology continues to develop, the benefits could significantly reduce hunger and malnutrition, transforming areas once considered food deserts into thriving agricultural hubs. You can see how interconnected these technologies are, with solutions in one area enhancing possibilities in another.

But the impact of innovation doesn't stop there. On the horizon, quantum computing stands ready to shatter barriers that have held back traditional computers for ages. While regular computers work using a system of ones and zeros, quantum computers use quantum bits, or qubits, which can represent multiple values at once. This means they can handle enormous amounts of data and solve complicated problems at lightning speed. The potential applications are mind-blowing, ranging from drug discovery to secure communications.

For example, the pharmaceutical industry could experience a faster pace in developing life-saving drugs. By harnessing quantum computing, researchers can simulate how molecules interact on an unprecedented scale, helping them find solutions to diseases that have long evaded treatment. This technology might shorten the time it takes to bring new drugs to market, ultimately saving countless lives. In the realm of data protection, quantum computing could create unbreakable encryption, dramatically improving our digital security. The rapid advancements in speed and efficiency open doors to new possibilities across various industries.

The way biotechnology and quantum computing work together perfectly illustrates how different technological advancements can combine to create a wave of innovation. The magic lies in their connection—when one breakthrough enhances another, it creates a ripple effect of progress that can shape our society for generations. It's not just about these individual technologies; it's about how they can unite to offer solutions that push beyond traditional limits.

As we look toward the future, the pressing global challenges we face—like climate change, food security, and healthcare—inspire us to collaborate. No single nation can tackle these problems alone. In our increasingly interconnected world, the success of one nation's innovations can benefit another. This reinforces the need for international cooperation, as the global nature of these issues calls for a united front where knowledge, resources, and breakthroughs flow across borders to uplift everyone.

Imagine the possibilities of a joint effort to create sustainable energy solutions. Countries rich in renewable resources could share their technologies and findings with those who aren't as fortunate. By learning from each other's successes and failures, we can build a stronger foundation for sustainable growth. Picture solar technology developed in sunny areas being adapted for use in places that don't get as much sun, leading to effective energy solutions for everyone. This showcases not just the power of technology but also the vital importance of breaking down barriers that stop collaboration.

However, as we tap into these groundbreaking technologies, we must also stay aware of the ethical concerns that arise. Conversations about biotechnology and AI have shown that our advancements should be guided by moral values. As we dive into quantum computing and renewable energy, we must ensure that our push for progress doesn't come at the cost of ethical standards. Finding a balance between innovation and responsibility is key. This is where international teamwork can play a vital role, as shared ethical guidelines can help uphold values like transparency, fairness, and sustainability.

As we move forward, we need to create an atmosphere that supports collaboration and innovation across all sectors. This isn't just a job for scientists and tech experts; it's a social responsibility that calls for involvement from educators, policymakers, and everyday citizens. The challenge lies in nurturing an environment where ideas can grow freely, enriched by diverse perspectives and experiences. The more inclusive our discussions, the more likely we are to develop comprehensive solutions to urgent global issues.

In this era of rapid technological growth, we must also be aware that these innovations can highlight societal inequalities. The digital divide continues to exist, leaving marginalized communities behind in this race for progress. To prevent widening these gaps, we must prioritize fair access to emerging technologies. By investing in education and infrastructure, we can empower individuals and communities to participate in this technological renaissance, ensuring that no one is left behind.

Moving ahead isn't just about making technological strides; it's also about fostering a culture where innovation and responsibility go hand in hand. As we navigate the complexities of biotechnology, quantum computing, and renewable energy, we should strive for sensible regulations that encourage exploration while protecting ethical standards. This calls for the involvement of a diverse range of stakeholders, each bringing their unique insights to craft a flexible and comprehensive regulatory environment.

In the end, the message is clear: we need to embrace a vision where countries and communities collaborate to harness technology for the greater good. The stakes are high. By looking beyond our immediate interests, we can tackle global challenges head-on and lay the groundwork for a sustainable and thriving future.

Imagine a world where we combine the strengths of AI, biotechnology, quantum computing, and renewable energy to elevate humanity. In this vision, global leaders, researchers, and communities unite in a shared mission, breaking down the barriers that have long separated us. The solutions are within reach; all we need is a commitment to collaborate, share knowledge, and foster innovations that benefit everyone.

Ultimately, we have the chance to rewrite the story of technological progress. This narrative shouldn't be told only in terms of competition and isolation but in the language of cooperation and shared success. We are standing on the edge of a new era, where the lines between technologies blur, creating a landscape ripe for innovation that addresses the world's greatest challenges. This isn't just a dream—it's a real possibility, and it's up to us to make it happen.

Innovation Without Limits

In the rapidly changing world of technology, the clash between rules and creativity is a hot topic that many people are talking about. It's a tricky situation, where our need for safety and ethical guidelines often runs into the wish for limitless creativity and progress. On one side, we want to keep our communities safe from any unexpected problems that new technologies might bring; on the other side, we don't want to hold back the very breakthroughs that could lead us to a better future. This tricky balance is where the idea of "Innovation Without Limits" comes into play, pushing for rules that help rather than hinder technological exploration.

When we take a closer look at the current regulations, it's easy to see that they can sometimes be a mixed bag. Rules are created with good intentions—mainly to protect public health, maintain ethical standards, and care for our environment. But there are times when these regulations can unintentionally slow down progress, making it harder for new ideas to take flight. Many innovators find themselves tangled in red tape, which can lead to frustration and missed opportunities.

Imagine a brilliant scientist who's come up with a groundbreaking invention that could change the world. They might find themselves stuck in a maze of regulations that make it tough to get their idea off the ground. While we definitely want to keep our society safe, it's vital that we also encourage creativity and new solutions. Finding ways to simplify regulations without compromising safety can create a more welcoming environment for innovation.

The key lies in creating a balanced approach—one that fosters growth while keeping safety as a priority. This means working together: lawmakers, innovators, and the public need to have open conversations about how we can support new ideas while also ensuring that they are safe and ethical. By doing this, we can create a future where technology can thrive without losing sight of our values.

In this ongoing conversation, it's crucial to remember that innovation and regulation don't have to be at odds. Instead, they can work hand in hand, paving the way for advancements that benefit us all. Embracing the mindset of "Innovation Without Limits" can lead us to a world where we harness the power of technology responsibly, unlocking new possibilities while staying true to our commitment to safety and ethics.

Chapter 5: Embracing the Kardashev Ambition

Scaling Civilization

In the story of humanity, civilization is often measured by how well we adapt, innovate, and grow. Throughout history, we've explored tremendous landscapes, built intricate societies, and uncovered the secrets of our universe. Yet here we are, standing on the edge of a new chapter that calls for our immediate attention and action. The Kardashev scale, created by Russian astrophysicist Nikolai Kardashev, provides a fascinating way to understand our progress. This scale ranks civilizations by their energy use, starting with Type I, which uses the energy of its own planet, moving to Type II, which can harness energy from stars, and finally to Type III, which can manipulate energy on a galactic scale. Right now, we find ourselves just on the verge of Type I, with an urgent need to shift gears from slowing down to speeding up.

This transformation is more urgent than ever. Our current path, filled with complacency and rigid ideas, threatens not just our survival but also the chance for our civilization to truly thrive. We face unprecedented challenges: climate change, resource depletion, and social inequalities loom large, casting shadows over our hopes. However, the answer is within our grasp if we embrace the Kardashev vision, which encourages technological progress and teamwork.

To move our civilization toward Type I, we first need to tackle the obstacles that hold us back. Sticking to old habits and being afraid to try new methods often blocks our progress. Many people are held back by fear of the unknown, while others may simply not realize the incredible potential of technology to change things for the better. As we look toward a brighter future, we must understand that the change we desire won't happen by itself. It requires a united effort from individuals, businesses, and governments—a collective awakening that puts innovation, sustainability, and true engagement at the forefront.

One of the most crucial steps we need to take is to switch to renewable energy sources. Using solar, wind, and geothermal power is not just a choice; it's a necessity. We need to take full advantage of the abundant energy that our planet provides, rather than clinging to the fossil fuels of the past. This shift isn't just about technology; it's about changing our mindset too. We need to redefine how we see energy—focusing on sustainability and responsibility. As we envision the future, we should see ourselves as builders of an energy-efficient world, weighing the environmental impact of our choices against the benefits.

In this important mission, every single person has a vital role to play. Small actions we take each day can come together to create a powerful wave of change. Whether it's reducing our consumption or pushing for sustainable practices in our communities, each of us can contribute to the momentum needed to move society forward. Grassroots movements driven by passionate individuals can spark significant changes in public policy and business behavior. As we work together to build a culture of innovation, we should foster conversations and collaborations that cross boundaries—whether they are geographical, ideological, or institutional.

Businesses also play a crucial part in this shift. Corporations have the power to shape vast networks of people and resources. By making sustainable practices a priority and investing in the latest technologies, they can drive real change. Many forward-thinking companies are starting to see the importance of weaving environmental concerns into their core strategies. They are adopting circular economies, aiming to reduce waste and use resources more efficiently, ultimately rethinking what success really means. The corporate world is at a turning point where aligning profit with purpose can shape their legacy for generations to come.

Governments need to step up too. We need policies that encourage the use of renewable energy, support research in sustainable technologies, and promote care for the environment as we work toward a Type I civilization. Global cooperation is crucial; in our interconnected world, no nation can succeed alone. By building international partnerships and committing to shared goals, we can strengthen our efforts and speed up progress. However, agreements and treaties must come with a real commitment to action—not just words. The urgency of the challenges we face demands tangible results.

As we navigate this intricate landscape, it's important to remember that moving toward a Type I civilization is about more than just energy consumption; it's about what it truly means to be human. Our ability to create, innovate, and work together is what defines us. Space exploration reminds us of our natural desire to reach for the unknown. By looking to the stars, we not only expand our understanding of the universe but also inspire future generations to dream big, think creatively, and strive for progress.

Our quest for a Type I civilization holds implications far beyond our own planet. The challenges we encounter today—climate change, resource shortages, and social inequality—are not impossible to overcome. When we gaze into the cosmos, we find that our hopes for a sustainable, prosperous future resonate with the very core of the universe. The universe invites us to reach out, innovate, and embrace the endless possibilities that lie ahead.

By creating a culture that values science, welcomes technological advancements, and puts the well-being of everyone first, we can unlock the doors to a brighter future. The road ahead may be filled with challenges, but with determination and unity, we can elevate civilization to heights we've only dreamed of. The Kardashev ambition isn't just a destination; it's a guiding principle encouraging us to tap into our collective potential and build a legacy of hope and progress for those who come after us.

As we wrap up this chapter, let's remember that the journey toward becoming a Type I civilization isn't something we can do alone. It's a shared call to action, a reminder that together we can rise above the limitations of our current situation. We have the power to shape our future, redefine our relationship with energy and our environment, and nurture a culture that celebrates innovation and sustainability. The future isn't far off; it's a reality waiting for us to create it. It's time to take hold of the Kardashev ambition and start a journey that will lead us to a more prosperous and harmonious life. The stars are not only our destination—they remind us of what we can achieve when we dare to dream and act.

Aspiring to Greatness

Aspiring to greatness means recognizing the incredible potential within each of us and in our shared journey as human beings. As we find ourselves on the edge of a new chapter in history, the Kardashev scale provides not only a way to understand how civilizations use energy but also a hopeful look at our future. We need to take real, practical steps toward reaching the goal of becoming a

Type I civilization. This isn't just a distant dream—it's something we must urgently pursue. The world is calling out for our attention and our actions if we want to turn our hopes into reality.

At the core of this change is the urgent need for an energy revolution. We must move away from fossil fuels—something we've relied on for ages but which is now harming our planet. Transitioning to renewable energy sources like solar, wind, hydroelectric, and geothermal isn't just a choice; it's crucial for our survival and growth. Picture using sunshine to power our lives, wind to generate electricity, and the Earth's heat to meet our energy needs. These resources are plentiful and can last indefinitely, yet our current systems often struggle to keep up with these fundamental changes.

The amazing technological progress we're seeing in energy storage and smart grids is exciting and could change the way we use energy. With better battery technology, we can save energy generated during sunny or breezy days and use it when we need it. This can solve many of the issues that often come with renewable energy sources. Plus, the rise of decentralized energy systems gives us a fresh alternative to the traditional energy grid. When local communities take charge of generating their own energy, they create a system that is not only more resilient but also fairer and more adaptable.

For the vision of a Type I civilization to succeed, we need strong systems for managing our resources sustainably. Our planet has limited resources, and it's on us to make sure we use them wisely. Innovative approaches in agriculture can really change how we think about food production. Methods like permaculture and vertical farming can grow food in a more sustainable way while using less land and water. This helps tackle the pressing issues of food security and environmental damage. By investing in practices that restore our soil and increase biodiversity, we can grow the food needed to support a rising population.

Water conservation is also a vital part of managing our resources. With more people needing fresh water, and with sources shrinking due to pollution and climate change, we must take action. By setting up rainwater harvesting systems, using water-efficient technologies, and restoring wetlands, we can greatly improve our water security. The combination of smart technology and natural solutions offers a promising way to manage this precious resource effectively.

 We can't overlook the importance of how we handle waste, either. The idea of a circular economy flips the old "take, make, dispose" model on its head. Instead, it encourages us to think differently about how we produce things and deal with waste. By focusing on recycling, composting, and upcycling, we can turn waste into valuable resources. Companies that adopt these circular practices find new ways to generate income while also reducing their environmental footprint. How we manage waste can reshape our relationship with consumption and production, helping us move toward a more sustainable future.

 However, individuals and businesses can't bring about this change on their own. Governments play a key role in creating an environment where innovation can thrive. Policies that encourage green technologies, support research and development, and fund educational programs focused on sustainability can lay down a strong foundation for progress. By creating rules that promote renewable energy usage, we can push for a shift towards cleaner technologies. Tax breaks for companies that practice sustainability can spark innovation and investment in green solutions.

Imagine a world where governments put sustainability at the top of their agenda, where protecting the environment isn't just an afterthought but a core value. This requires a commitment to being transparent and accountable, ensuring that policies result in real improvements. International cooperation is essential, as no single country can tackle these global issues alone. Agreements must lead to real actions that foster collaboration across borders.

Engaging communities is also crucial in our quest for greatness. Grassroots movements can bring about significant change from the ground up. Think about the impact of local projects that support community gardens, renewable energy cooperatives, or environmental clean-up efforts. These initiatives, often driven by passionate individuals, can rally support from the public and influence local laws. When people unite—regardless of their differences—amazing transformations can occur.

The strength of collective action is incredible. When communities come together to advocate for sustainable practices, their efforts can create waves of change that affect larger organizations. The Transition Town movement is a perfect example of this. Starting in the UK, this grassroots initiative empowers communities to tackle climate change by boosting local resilience and self-sufficiency. As neighborhoods collaborate to share resources and skills, they foster a feeling of belonging and purpose, reinforcing that change often starts from our own backyards.

A well-known example of a grassroots movement pushing for environmental justice highlights how communities of color and low-income areas often face the worst of pollution and environmental harm. Activists in these regions have banded together to demand cleaner air and water, often overcoming significant challenges. By organizing, educating, and advocating for their rights, they have not only improved their own neighborhoods but also sparked wider conversations about fairness and justice in environmental policies.

All around the world, we see numerous examples of how teamwork among individuals, businesses, and governments can create real change. The rise of urban agriculture projects in cities like Detroit and Havana shows how communities can take back vacant land to produce food, cut down on waste, and build social connections. These initiatives prove that sustainability isn't just a concept; it can become a reality that changes lives for the better.

As we move forward, let's remember that aspiring to greatness means fostering a vision that is inclusive and fair. Transitioning to a Type I civilization isn't just about technology or energy use; it's about building a world where everyone can flourish. It involves breaking down barriers that have sidelined certain groups and ensuring all voices are included in important decisions. By valuing diversity and inclusion, we can create a stronger, more innovative society that taps into the unique strengths of all its members.

The challenges we face are significant, but they also give us a chance to change how we interact with each other and with our planet. The vision of a Type I civilization encourages us to dream big and expand what we believe is possible. The goal of using our planet's energy sustainably isn't just a technological challenge; it requires a change in our values and priorities. It asks us to cultivate a culture that celebrates working together, creativity, and responsibility.

On this journey toward greatness, every little effort matters. Individuals can choose actions that align with their values—like reducing energy use, supporting local businesses, or pushing for sustainable policies. Companies can rethink their operations, integrate environmental considerations into their core missions, and invest in technologies that promote sustainability. Governments can lead by example, create supportive frameworks, and work with communities to develop solutions together.

Ultimately, striving for greatness is about sparking a movement—a movement that crosses boundaries, awakens our shared awareness, and drives us toward a brighter future. The Kardashev ambition isn't just an individual quest; it's a call for unity, creativity, and collaboration. Together, we can rise to meet the challenges of our time, showing that our greatest potential lies not only in technological progress but in our ability to unite as caretakers of our planet.

As we navigate the complexities of this transition, let's stay committed to building a sustainable and fair future. Our dreams of a Type I civilization are within reach, but we can only achieve them through collective effort, shared goals, and a steadfast pursuit of greatness. The road may be tough, but with determination, innovation, and unity, we can create a world where prosperity, well-being, and harmony thrive— a world that reflects the best of our humanity.

Our Destiny Among the Stars

When we look up at the night sky, it's hard not to feel a sense of wonder and excitement. The stars that shine so brightly are more than just distant balls of gas; they embody our hopes and dreams as a species. Right now, we stand at the edge of a new era filled with amazing technology, challenges brought by climate change, and a booming population. The vast universe around us holds endless possibilities just waiting for us to reach out and explore. Our journey into the stars isn't just poetic; it's a crucial step for the survival and growth of humanity.

Space exploration has been a game changer, shaping the world we live in today. Think about the satellites spinning around the Earth. They help us communicate globally, predict the weather, and even find our way using smartphones. These incredible inventions came from our desire to discover what lies beyond our planet. The same creativity that pushes us into space also leads to innovations that make our everyday lives better. For example, techniques developed for space are now used in medical imaging, and breakthroughs in materials science are changing industries. Our adventures in space have a lasting impact on life back home.

But the quest to explore space isn't just about technology; it also brings people together. When we gaze at the stars, we're reminded of our shared humanity and the challenges we all face. We're all living on this delicate blue planet, orbiting a yellow star at the edge of a spiral galaxy. Yet, our curiosity drives us to explore the unknown. This urge to question our existence and push boundaries is what makes us human. Exploring space allows us to seek answers to some of life's biggest questions: Who are we? Where did we come from? And what does the future hold for us?

To secure our future, we need to think beyond Earth's limits. The resources on our planet are finite, and they can't support our growing population and consumption forever. Looking to space offers a chance to access resources beyond our world, which could help us tackle issues of scarcity. For instance, mining asteroids or using the Moon for industry could provide us with important materials, like rare metals, that are crucial in today's tech-driven age. This not only eases the strain on Earth but also opens doors for economic growth and new opportunities.

Picture this: a future where the Moon serves as a launching pad for deeper exploration of our Solar System. With its lower gravity and rich resources, lunar bases could become centers for research and manufacturing. By using materials from the Moon, we could build spacecraft to explore Mars and beyond. This isn't just a dream; it's within our reach. The Artemis program, aiming to return humans to the Moon by the mid-2020s, is a big step toward this goal. Establishing a sustainable presence on the Moon will give us valuable experience and knowledge, laying the groundwork for future adventures in space.

However, we can't ignore the ethical questions that come with space colonization. As we stretch our reach into the cosmos, we need to think about our responsibilities—not just to each other here on Earth, but also to the environments we encounter. The lessons we've learned in caring for our planet should guide our actions in space. We must resist the temptation to exploit resources without considering the consequences. Instead, we should explore other worlds with a mindset of respect and responsibility, making sure our actions benefit both humanity and the environments we hope to inhabit.

The spirit of exploration is part of what makes us human. The stories of astronauts who have ventured into the unknown inspire us and resonate deeply. They remind us of our ability to dream big and envision a future beyond the limitations of our current reality. When astronauts look back at Earth from space, they often talk about feeling a profound sense of connection and unity, witnessing the delicate beauty of our planet suspended in the vastness around us. This perspective highlights that we are part of a larger story—a story that calls for collaboration, empathy, and a shared commitment to caring for our home.

The idea of a Type I civilization, according to the Kardashev scale, challenges us to harness all the energy our planet has to offer—a goal that also invites us to look beyond Earth. As we evolve into this advanced civilization, we could learn to use resources from not just our planet but also other celestial bodies. This ambition isn't only about technology; it's about ensuring the survival of our species in the face of potential dangers. By mastering resource use on the Moon, Mars, and possibly other planets, we can create a safety net for humanity against disasters that might threaten our home.

The stakes are high, yet the opportunities are endless. As we push further into space, we must cultivate a sense of responsibility for both our planet and the greater universe. This balance between exploration and preservation calls on us to be wise stewards of our actions in space. We should seek knowledge and resources without harming the environments we encounter. We need to learn from our past on Earth and use that wisdom to guide our future in space.

While we chase our dreams among the stars, we also need to think about the philosophical and ethical questions that come with space colonization. Who gets to explore and settle on other worlds? This raises important issues of fairness and justice. As we create new technologies and policies for space travel, it's essential to ensure that the benefits are shared by everyone, not just a select few. The spirit of cooperation that has driven international missions—like those to the International Space Station—should be our guiding light as we extend our reach into the cosmos. By working together across borders and cultures, we can ensure that our journey into space embodies the values of inclusion and shared purpose.

Additionally, exploring space can ignite a sense of wonder and curiosity in younger generations. By encouraging interest in science, technology, engineering, and mathematics (STEM), we can inspire a new wave of explorers, thinkers, and problem solvers ready to tackle the challenges ahead. Space exploration is a fantastic platform to spark young minds, helping them imagine a future filled with opportunities. By investing in education and outreach programs focused on space, we not only prepare future leaders but also cultivate a culture of curiosity and innovation.

Pursuing the ambition of becoming a Type I civilization isn't just about reaching for the stars; it also calls us to acknowledge the connections between our goals here at home. Building a sustainable future requires a balanced approach that combines technological progress with social and environmental responsibility. The challenges we face—like climate change and resource shortages—can motivate us to innovate and collaborate. As we work together toward becoming a Type I civilization, we can harness our collective strength to make a lasting difference.

The path to our destiny among the stars will have its difficulties, but it's also filled with hope and potential. Every step we take to understand and explore the cosmos brings us closer to achieving our biggest dreams. By pursuing space exploration as a way to advance our civilization and tackle urgent problems here on Earth, we create a brighter future for those who will come after us.

In this grand journey, each person plays an important role. Each of us can contribute to this movement, whether through education, advocacy, or innovation. By embracing our shared connections, we can amplify our impact and inspire others to join us in this transformative adventure. Together, we can foster a sense of urgency and optimism, reminding ourselves that the cosmos is not just a distant frontier but a treasure trove of possibilities waiting to be explored.

Ultimately, our destiny among the stars reflects humanity's resilience, creativity, and quest for discovery. It's a call to action—a chance for us to recognize our potential and take charge of our responsibilities as caretakers of our planet and the universe. By striving to become a Type I civilization, we can secure a thriving and sustainable future for generations yet to come. This journey isn't only about the technology we create or resources we gather; it's about the legacy we leave behind and the values we embrace as we reach for the stars.

As we navigate the complexities of our lives on this planet, let's not lose sight of the vast universe that surrounds us. The stars invite us to dream, to explore, and to connect with something greater than ourselves. In doing this, we honor the beauty of our world and the limitless possibilities waiting for us among the stars, ultimately paving the way to a brighter and more sustainable future for all of humanity.

Cornel Jefferson

Chapter 6: The Power of Bold Entrepreneurship

Catalysts of Change

In a world where settling for the status quo is all too common, some remarkable individuals step up and shake things up with their daring ideas and fearless visions. These pioneers, often called bold entrepreneurs, combine resilience, creativity, and a never-ending thirst for innovation. They aren't just business people; they are change-makers who inspire generations to rethink what's possible. As we look into what it means to be a bold entrepreneur, we'll uncover the key traits that define these visionaries and explore the meaningful projects they've brought to life. Their journeys not only show the potential for real change in society but also offer valuable insights for aspiring entrepreneurs who dream big.

At the core of any bold entrepreneur is a strong belief in their vision. This inner drive pushes them to challenge the norm and aim for breakthroughs that can transform entire industries. Take Elon Musk, for example. His impressive career spans several fields, and he's become a symbol of innovation and disruption.

While his companies, like Tesla and SpaceX, may seem different at first glance, they share a common purpose: tackling some of the biggest challenges we face today. Musk didn't just jump into electric vehicles for profit; he saw a vital need to fight climate change. By changing the automotive landscape and advocating for sustainable energy, he has sparked a cultural shift toward caring for our planet, showing that bold entrepreneurs can use technology to build a greener future.

Similarly, Sara Blakely's path to creating Spanx highlights the power of creativity and entrepreneurship. With her fresh take on women's undergarments, Blakely completely changed a market that had been stuck in old-fashioned ideals and restrictive designs. Her determination and grit didn't just shake up the fashion industry; they also empowered countless women by promoting body positivity and self-love. Blakely's story emphasizes the importance of spotting gaps in the market and seizing opportunities that others might miss. She proves that sometimes the simplest ideas, when driven by authenticity and a real understanding of what people want, can lead to monumental change.

The efforts of these bold entrepreneurs leave a lasting impact that reaches far beyond their own fields. Musk's push for electric vehicles is part of a larger movement toward sustainable transportation, inspiring governments, businesses, and individuals to rethink their reliance on fossil fuels. We can see this cultural shift in the growing number of people advocating for eco-friendly practices and policies that prioritize the health of our planet. Blakely's influence goes beyond fashion; her success story resonates with aspiring entrepreneurs everywhere, showing that with determination, creativity, and a strong belief in oneself, anything is possible.

Looking closer at the lives of these inspiring figures, we can uncover valuable lessons for the next wave of entrepreneurs. One key takeaway is the importance of resilience when facing challenges. Both Musk and Blakely have encountered their share of failures and doubt along the way. Musk, for instance, faced many hurdles while launching SpaceX, including rocket failures and money troubles. Yet, his unwavering commitment to his vision kept him going. Likewise, Blakely faced numerous rejections from manufacturers before she finally found someone who believed in her idea. Their experiences remind us that the road to success isn't always smooth and that resilience is a vital trait for any bold entrepreneur.

Creativity is also a crucial part of the entrepreneurial toolkit. Bold entrepreneurs like Musk and Blakely see challenges not as obstacles but as chances to innovate. Their knack for thinking outside the box and creating solutions that defy conventional wisdom is what makes them stand out. For those looking to start their own ventures, embracing creativity can lead to groundbreaking ideas that disrupt industries and spark movements. Ultimately, being willing to experiment, learn from failures, and keep evolving is what helps develop an entrepreneurial mindset ready to face an ever-changing landscape.

As we reflect on the journeys of these remarkable individuals, it becomes clear that bold entrepreneurship can drive significant change in society. The initiatives led by visionaries like Musk and Blakely illustrate how innovation can tackle pressing issues and reshape entire industries. These stories aren't just about individual achievements; they represent a shared hope for a brighter future—

one fueled by imagination, resilience, and a commitment to making a positive impact.

At its heart, bold entrepreneurship is built on the belief that anyone can be a catalyst for change. The paths taken by these trailblazers inspire aspiring entrepreneurs to tap into their creativity, confront their fears, and chase their visions with passion. As we continue to explore the transformative power of bold entrepreneurs, it's important to recognize how their work influences society and the lessons we can take from their journeys. With the right mindset and support, anyone can embrace the spirit of entrepreneurship and help drive the innovation that leads humanity toward a better and more prosperous future.

Ultimately, it's not just about the entrepreneurs themselves; it's about the movement they inspire. By challenging norms and encouraging others to unleash their entrepreneurial spirit, they create a ripple effect that crosses industries and borders. This shared momentum is what truly fuels societal change, proving that bold entrepreneurship is more than just a personal quest; it's a powerful force capable of reshaping the world.

Disrupting the Status Quo

Disruption is a concept that can feel like a double-edged sword. On one hand, it brings innovation, pushing businesses to grow and adapt or face decline. On the other hand, it can create dramatic changes that shake established companies to their core, leaving them scrambling to catch up. In the business world, disruption refers to a process where smaller companies with fewer resources successfully challenge larger, established firms—often by focusing on ignored markets or introducing new technologies that completely change the industry. This isn't just a trend; it's a vital part of our economic system, responsible for many of the significant changes in how consumers behave and how industries operate.

To really understand the impact of disruption, let's look at some relatable examples. One of the most telling stories is the rise and fall of Blockbuster, paired with the growth of Netflix. Blockbuster, once the giant in the movie rental business, perfectly illustrates a company that didn't adapt to shifting consumer preferences. In the late 1990s and early 2000s, while Blockbuster was busy opening more stores and cashing in on late fees, Netflix quietly entered the scene with a game-changing idea: online DVD rentals. This wasn't just a small tweak; it was a complete overhaul of how people accessed entertainment.

But Netflix didn't stop there. The company made a daring move into streaming services, which not only changed how audiences watched movies and TV shows but also transformed the entire entertainment landscape. They paid attention to what consumers wanted and recognized the growing need for convenience—people were tired of waiting in line to rent DVDs. Netflix's strategy wasn't just about offering a faster option; it was about creating a whole new way to enjoy entertainment that fit the busy lives of modern viewers. People wanted on-demand access to content they could watch anytime, anywhere, on any device.

The results were staggering. By the time Blockbuster tried to shift to a digital model, it was already too late. The company had crumbled under the weight of a market it once ruled. In 2010, Blockbuster filed for bankruptcy, while Netflix thrived, eventually becoming a major producer of its own content and a global leader in entertainment. This story captures the essence of disruption: a smaller player spotting an opportunity and using technology to meet not just the existing demand but also to create new demand in ways that had never been seen before.

Now, let's look at how disruption has reshaped the hospitality industry with Airbnb. Founded in 2008 by Brian Chesky, Nathan Blecharczyk, and Joe Gebbia, Airbnb started with a simple idea: to give travelers a unique and affordable option compared to traditional hotels. Initially, the idea of renting out spare rooms or entire homes to strangers raised eyebrows. However, by tapping into the growing sharing economy and the internet, Airbnb quickly gained popularity.

What set Airbnb apart was its ability to disrupt a long-standing industry by appealing to the desire for genuine experiences. Travelers weren't just looking for a place to crash; they were eager to dive into local culture. By using technology to link homeowners with guests, Airbnb created a platform that offered not only budget-friendly lodging but also a chance for guests to experience cities like a local. This new approach changed the travel accommodation landscape, intensifying competition for traditional hotels, which were often seen as bland and uniform.

The ripple effects of Airbnb's disruption reached far and wide. Cities around the world began facing challenges related to the surge in short-term rentals—issues like housing shortages, zoning conflicts, and the impact on local neighborhoods became major concerns. Traditional hotels had to step up their game, introducing unique features and personalized services to keep their customers. Many hotel chains started to incorporate aspects of the Airbnb model into their offerings as they rethought their strategies.

The consequences of these disruptions go beyond just shaking up the market. They often lead to a new way of thinking about what consumers expect and what industries should deliver. The emergence of Netflix and Airbnb has not only provided alternatives to traditional services but also raised the bar for what people now demand. Whether it's the ease of streaming on demand or the longing for personalized travel experiences, these companies have fundamentally changed how industries work and how consumers engage with services.

When we think about the larger implications of disruption, it's clear that it creates an environment ripe for competition and innovation. More competition usually leads to better services and lower prices, as companies strive to meet the changing needs of their customers. This shift towards focusing on the consumer can be seen as a direct result of bold entrepreneurship—a movement that pushes boundaries and inspires others to innovate.

Moreover, the spirit of disruption can energize entire sectors of society. It creates a space where taking risks is encouraged and where creativity is celebrated. Entrepreneurs are motivated to think outside the box and try new things without the fear of failing paralyzing them. The journeys of Netflix and Airbnb not only resonate within their industries but also act as inspiring examples for the next generation of entrepreneurs.

Building a culture that welcomes disruption is vital for creating an environment where innovation can thrive. Policymakers, educators, and business leaders need to work together to foster a mindset that values experimentation, recognizing that failure is just a step along the path to success. This can be accomplished through supportive policies for startups, investments in technology, and promoting creativity and entrepreneurial thinking in education.

To truly embrace disruption, society must actively recognize and nurture the power of fresh ideas, especially in a world that is more interconnected than ever. This means seeking out new inventions, welcoming diverse viewpoints, and celebrating those who dare to challenge the status quo.

In the bigger picture of entrepreneurship, disruptive innovators remind us that change is not only achievable but necessary. Their stories light the way toward a brighter future—one where innovation is the standard, not the exception. By adopting a forward-thinking attitude, anyone can join the wave of disruption, turning their ideas into real solutions that promote progress.

Ultimately, the tales of Netflix, Airbnb, and many other disruptors reveal a key truth about entrepreneurship: it flourishes when we question established norms and dream of a future that breaks away from tradition. By nurturing a culture that celebrates bold innovation, we can unlock the potential for transformative change across industries—one venture at a time.

Creating an Ecosystem for Success

The world of entrepreneurship resembles a lively garden, full of diverse plants and flowers that thrive through mutual support and interaction. To truly grasp how to build and nurture successful businesses, we need to understand what an entrepreneurial ecosystem is. This ecosystem isn't just a random collection of businesses and investors; it's a lively mix of different elements that work together to spark new ideas and fuel economic growth. Entrepreneurs, investors, schools, and government policies all come together to create a setting where bold ideas can flourish and entrepreneurial dreams can take flight.

At its heart, an entrepreneurial ecosystem is all about supporting people and organizations on their journey to success. Imagine a garden where soil, water, sunlight, and nutrients work hand in hand to create a vibrant landscape. With proper care, that garden produces beautiful flowers and delicious fruits. The same goes for an entrepreneurial ecosystem—it flourishes when the key players work together, share resources, and build a culture that welcomes risk and creativity. The most successful ecosystems attract talent and resources, encourage experimentation, and foster a sense of community among entrepreneurs.

A key feature of a strong entrepreneurial ecosystem is its ability to provide access to funding. In the early days of a startup, money is often what keeps the idea alive. Without enough funding, even the best ideas can fade away. So, a successful ecosystem makes sure entrepreneurs can tap into various funding sources like venture capital, angel investors, crowdfunding, and government grants. Each of these funding avenues is important for helping startups take risks, grow their operations, and carve out a space in the market.

Networking opportunities are also crucial for spurring innovation within an ecosystem. Entrepreneurs thrive on connections—whether it's with fellow innovators, mentors, or industry experts. Events like networking gatherings, conferences, and meetups allow entrepreneurs to share ideas, build partnerships, and seek guidance from those who have been through similar challenges. Networking has a special way of igniting collaboration, enabling entrepreneurs to draw on each other's strengths and insights. Plus, these connections often lead to mentorship programs where experienced entrepreneurs guide newcomers, helping them navigate common hurdles and fast-track their growth.

Educational institutions play a vital role in supporting entrepreneurial ecosystems too. Colleges and universities are more than just places of learning; they are hotbeds for innovation and creativity. By fostering an entrepreneurial culture on campus, schools can give students the skills and mindset they need to succeed in the business world. This can be done through courses focused on entrepreneurship, incubators, and accelerators that help students turn their ideas into real businesses. When educational institutions collaborate with local businesses, they can create paths for students to gain hands-on experience and encourage a spirit of innovation in their communities.

Government policies are also key in shaping the entrepreneurial landscape. Supportive regulations can make a huge difference in nurturing startups and encouraging innovation. Governments can introduce policies that offer tax breaks for new businesses, grants for research and development, and initiatives that cut down on red tape. By removing barriers, policymakers can empower entrepreneurs to take chances and chase their dreams without being bogged down by complicated processes. Additionally, governments can promote entrepreneurship through public campaigns that highlight the successes of local innovators and inspire future generations of entrepreneurs.

However, it's not just about the structures and systems in place; the way a society views entrepreneurship plays a huge role too. A culture that celebrates risk-taking and innovation is more likely to produce successful entrepreneurs than one that shuns failure. Societies that see entrepreneurship as a worthy pursuit create an environment where people feel encouraged to follow their ideas and take calculated risks. These cultural attitudes can be shaped through storytelling—sharing the journeys of entrepreneurs who have triumphed against the odds can motivate others to take similar paths. When failure is viewed not as a dead end but as a stepping stone to success, individuals are more likely to embrace daring ideas and venture into the unknown.

We can see the impact of cultural attitudes in places like Silicon Valley and Tel Aviv, which are known for their innovation and entrepreneurial spirit. In Silicon Valley, the drive for success fuels a continuous cycle of creativity and experimentation. The community is known for treating failure as a valuable lesson, fostering a culture where entrepreneurs feel free to take risks. Local investors often back promising concepts, understanding that not every attempt will succeed right away. This mindset has led to a thriving ecosystem where groundbreaking companies like Apple, Google, and Facebook have emerged.

Tel Aviv, too, has become a global startup hub, driven by a vibrant culture of innovation. In a country that has faced its share of challenges, the entrepreneurial spirit shines brightly, turning adversity into opportunity. Israeli entrepreneurs are celebrated for their creativity and resilience. The government plays a supportive role by promoting research and development and encouraging collaboration between education and industry. As a result, Tel Aviv has become a breeding ground for cutting-edge technologies and startups, attracting talent and investment from all over the globe.

Looking at these successful ecosystems reveals several important elements that other regions aiming to create similar environments should consider. First, access to funding is crucial. Investors should be motivated to support startups through various financial options like equity, loans, and grants. Additionally, creating networking opportunities and mentorship programs can help build a sense of community among entrepreneurs, giving them the tools and support they need to thrive.

Educational institutions should also actively engage with the entrepreneurial ecosystem, designing programs that encourage students to think outside the box and pursue their entrepreneurial dreams. By integrating real-world experiences into their curriculums and providing resources for startups, schools can play a vital role in shaping the next generation of innovators.

Meanwhile, policymakers need to team up with entrepreneurs to develop regulations that lower bureaucratic barriers while fostering innovation. This might include simplifying business registration processes, streamlining tax codes, and setting clear guidelines for startups. By creating a supportive environment, governments can inspire entrepreneurs to take risks and chase their visions with confidence.

Finally, nurturing a culture that values entrepreneurship is key to building an ecosystem where innovation can flourish. This involves not just sharing success stories, but also normalizing discussions around failure and learning. When society embraces the idea that entrepreneurship is a journey with its highs and lows, individuals are more likely to take that leap of faith into the world of innovation.

Ultimately, creating an ecosystem for success isn't just about erecting structures or implementing policies; it's about cultivating a mindset that welcomes creativity, risk-taking, and collaboration. By recognizing how all these pieces fit together and working hand in hand to nurture an environment that fosters innovation, we can unlock the full potential of entrepreneurship and drive positive change in society.

As we envision the future, it's clear that bold entrepreneurship will be a key force for transformation. By tapping into innovative ideas and disruptive technologies, we have the chance to tackle pressing challenges and build a brighter future for everyone. Supporting and nurturing the ecosystem that uplifts entrepreneurship is vital in this effort. It's a responsibility we all share, requiring the involvement of individuals, businesses, educational institutions, and governments.

Through teamwork, support, and a shared vision, we can create a space where daring entrepreneurs can thrive, inspiring generations to follow in their footsteps. By fostering a culture that values risk-taking, creativity, and innovation, we can lay the groundwork for a brighter tomorrow—where today's dreams become the groundbreaking realities of the future. Together, we can move toward a future defined by progress, empowerment, and a steadfast belief in the power of entrepreneurship to unlock our full potential.

Cornel Jefferson

Chapter 7: Reimagining the Future of Work

Automation as Opportunity

Right now, the world of work is going through a huge change, and automation is right at the center of this shift. When people hear the word "automation," they might picture scary machines taking over, leaving workers feeling abandoned and hopeless. While it's understandable why many might feel this way, especially given how the media often portrays it, that view is off base. Instead of signaling the end, automation can be a golden opportunity that opens up new paths for creativity, job satisfaction, and personal growth in the workplace.

Think back to how the workforce has evolved throughout history. Remember the Industrial Revolution? At first, many were worried as machines started replacing manual jobs and changed economies around the world. People feared for their jobs. But the very changes that caused these fears led to the birth of new industries and roles that didn't even exist before. We saw the rise of jobs in engineering, design, and management springing forth from what once was. The key takeaway here is to see technological advancements not as threats but as stepping stones for human progress.

The argument for automation is strong. Research from the World Economic Forum shows that while automation may eliminate certain jobs, it's also set to create over 97 million new roles. Many of these roles are focused on creativity, problem-solving, and working with others. The jobs of the future will need tech skills, the ability to adapt, and a knack for innovation. This is an exciting message: instead of being spectators, we have the chance to step into a vibrant new field brimming with possibilities.

Take artificial intelligence, for instance. This technology isn't just about making things faster; it can enhance our abilities in amazing ways. From crunching numbers to crafting stories, AI can help us explore new avenues we might not have thought about before. Picture an architect using AI to try out different designs quickly or a healthcare worker using machine learning to analyze patient information and suggest tailored treatments. In these examples, automation allows workers to zero in on what truly matters—like creativity, critical thinking, and emotional understanding.

It frees them from repetitive tasks, letting them focus their energy on the forward-thinking work that drives progress.

The conversation about automation often misses the human side of things. It's not just about machines taking over jobs; it's about reshaping what work means and what we want to achieve as individuals. With everyday tasks being automated, we have a fantastic chance to rethink our roles in the workplace. The future isn't about sitting back while machines do our work; it's about rising to the challenge of expanding our skill sets to fit into a constantly changing world.

This change is already happening in various fields. In manufacturing, for example, robots haven't eliminated the need for human workers. Instead, they've created a demand for people who can design, program, and maintain these advanced machines. The focus has shifted from hard labor to exciting, intellectually engaging tasks, requiring a new type of worker who is tech-savvy and flexible. This trend is evident across all industries, from farming to customer service. The need for people who can adeptly use new technologies is on the rise, creating opportunities for individuals to learn new skills and pursue careers that align with their passions.

Plus, the move toward automation isn't just happening with big corporations or in wealthy countries. Small and medium-sized businesses (SMEs) around the world are also starting to embrace automation, unlocking the same potential for innovation and growth. These businesses tend to be more nimble and can quickly adapt to new technologies, positioning themselves to succeed in competitive markets. For entrepreneurs and small business owners, automation can help cut costs and boost productivity, leading to groundbreaking ideas that can transform local economies.

However, a vital part of successfully integrating automation into the workforce is our readiness to welcome change. For many, the thought of adapting to new technologies can be intimidating, especially for those who have spent years mastering traditional roles. But resisting change can lead to stagnation. Instead, we need to develop a mindset that welcomes flexibility and lifelong learning. By viewing automation as an opportunity rather than a threat, we can build a culture of resilience that prepares us for future challenges and possibilities.

Education has a crucial part to play in this transformation. As we look toward the future, it's important for schools and universities to keep up with technological advancements. Educational programs should focus not just on technical skills but also on critical thinking and creativity, enabling students to thrive in a world where automation is commonplace. Collaborations between schools and tech companies can provide students with hands-on experiences with emerging technologies, preparing them for the realities of tomorrow's job market.

At the end of the day, the discussion around automation should shift from fear to empowerment. Yes, there will be bumps in the road as we navigate this new era, but there will also be incredible opportunities for growth and innovation. Welcoming automation means welcoming the chance for transformation—both for ourselves and as a society.

As we move forward, the real question isn't whether automation will reshape the workforce, but how we'll respond to these changes. Our ability to adapt, learn, and innovate will determine the future of work.

Embracing the idea that automation is an opportunity can lead us on a transformative journey—one that opens doors to creativity, teamwork, and a more rewarding work life. As we stand at the beginning of this new chapter, we have a unique chance to take hold of the moment and create a future where technology helps us reach our true potential rather than holding us back.

New Frontiers of Employment

The world of work is changing fast, opening up a realm full of exciting possibilities. As we step into this new era, it's important to appreciate the wide range of opportunities that are popping up across different fields. These chances aren't just a result of new technologies; they highlight our ability to adapt and innovate as humans. The future of work isn't just about getting by amid changes in automation and digital technology; it's about thriving and flourishing in these new circumstances.

One of the most promising areas on the rise is renewable energy. With the global push toward sustainable practices, there's an increasing need for skilled workers who can make use of the sun, wind, and water. This field isn't limited to engineers building solar panels or wind turbines; it includes a whole variety of roles, from project management to policy advocacy. People working in renewable energy are not only focusing on technology but also on community involvement, ensuring that the shift to green energy is fair and accessible for everyone.

To shed more light on this, I chatted with Dr. Emma Torres, who is a leading expert in renewable energy policy. She shared, "The discussion about green jobs often focuses on the technical side, but we can't forget how crucial community engagement is. We need advocates who can connect with people, explain the benefits of renewable energy, and make sure everyone can access these new opportunities." Dr. Torres emphasizes that this transition to cleaner energy requires everyone's input. Skills like communication, empathy, and cultural understanding are just as vital as technical expertise.

Biotechnology is another field that is shaping our future jobs. With breakthroughs in gene editing and synthetic biology, new positions are emerging that blend biology with data analysis and ethical considerations. While scientists continue to push the limits of what's possible, they also have to navigate the moral challenges that come with their discoveries.

This intersection creates a demand for professionals who understand both the science and the ethical implications, ensuring that advancements benefit humanity rather than putting it at risk. Future jobs in biotechnology will need a mix of lab skills, data knowledge, and ethical reasoning—a combination that many educational programs are beginning to embrace.

We also can't overlook the significance of data science. As businesses and governments turn to data for making decisions and planning strategies, the demand for data analysts and scientists keeps growing. However, this field isn't just about crunching numbers; it requires a deep understanding of the context surrounding the data. Data professionals need to be able to draw meaningful insights that lead to practical solutions, making sure that data is a force for good. The way we talk about data science is shifting toward storytelling, where numbers turn into narratives that guide important choices in policy and business.

At the same time, the rise of artificial intelligence (AI) is changing job roles everywhere. While some people worry about AI taking jobs away, the reality is more complex. AI can actually enhance human abilities, helping professionals across various sectors work more efficiently. For instance, healthcare workers can use AI algorithms to diagnose diseases more quickly and accurately, while creative professionals can harness AI tools to elevate their artistic efforts. This brings about new hybrid roles where traditional skills are paired with tech savvy, resulting in a workforce that is more adaptable and versatile.

As we explore these new horizons in employment, it's vital to focus on developing our skills. The future job market will be defined by the need for flexibility and a commitment to lifelong learning. Workers will need to actively pursue new skills—through formal education, online courses, or hands-on training—to stay current in a constantly changing environment. Companies also have a role to play by investing in their employees' training and growth, creating a culture of ongoing improvement that benefits everyone and drives innovation.

Meanwhile, the gig economy has become an important part of this new work landscape. The flexibility that comes with freelancing and contract work is appealing to many, especially in a world where work-life balance is increasingly valued. Platforms connecting freelancers to clients are creating opportunities for individuals to build careers that suit their unique skills and lifestyles. However, the gig economy also raises important questions about job security, benefits, and protections for workers. As more people turn to freelance work, it's crucial to advocate for policies that ensure fair wages, health care, and other essential benefits for gig workers.

To gain a better understanding of the gig economy, I spoke with Sarah Kim, a freelance graphic designer who has successfully navigated the challenges of independent work. She said, "The freedom is amazing, but there are days when I worry about my financial situation. It's important to create a safety net for freelancers, whether that means health benefits or retirement plans." Sarah's insights underline the urgent need for a support system that empowers gig workers and enables them to succeed in their chosen paths.

As remote work continues to grow, we see a clear redefinition of the workplace. The traditional office isn't the only location for collaboration and productivity anymore. Remote work has freed people from geographical constraints, allowing companies to tap into talent from all over the world. This shift calls for a new approach to teamwork and communication, with a focus on digital collaboration tools and virtual engagement strategies.

However, remote work does come with its challenges. It demands a level of self-discipline and motivation that not everyone has. The blurred lines between work and home can lead to burnout if not handled properly. Organizations need to establish clear expectations and boundaries, fostering an environment that prioritizes employee well-being. Additionally, leaders must develop skills to manage remote teams effectively, making sure that employees feel connected and valued, no matter where they are located.

As we navigate these new frontiers of employment, we should take a comprehensive look at the workforce landscape. The intersections of technology, ethics, and humanity should guide our approach to tapping into the potential of emerging fields. This requires teamwork among industries, educational institutions, and policymakers to ensure we cultivate a workforce ready to thrive amid change.

The conversation about work is evolving; it's not just about tasks anymore, but about purpose and impact too. The jobs of the future will not only benefit individual prosperity but will also tackle global challenges like climate change, access to healthcare, and social equity. As workers, leaders, and innovators, we must embrace this transformation, realizing that we are not just parts of a machine but creators of a brighter future.

In this rapidly changing environment, we should ask ourselves not only what skills we need to learn but also how we can positively influence the world around us. The future of work relies not just on our ability to adapt but on our dedication to building a more just, equitable world for everyone. By harnessing technology, advocating for fair labor practices, and promoting a culture of continuous learning, we can reimagine work in a way that empowers individuals and strengthens communities. The new frontiers of employment invite us to rise to the challenge and pave the way for a future that's not just about jobs but about purpose, innovation, and the collective progress of humanity.

Empowering the Workforce

As we explore the challenges of a tech-driven economy, empowering our workforce through educational reform is more important than ever. This is an urgent topic that affects us all, and it demands our attention and action. Our current educational practices, which mostly come from the industrial age, just don't cut it anymore in a job market that is rapidly changing due to technology. Too often, graduates leave school feeling unprepared for the real-world challenges that await them. We find ourselves at a crucial moment, where we need to not only acknowledge the flaws in our educational systems but also imagine what a more responsive and relevant curriculum could look like.

When we take a close look at our current educational system, we uncover some worrying truths. Traditional teaching methods, while they may have worked in the past, often emphasize memorization and standardized tests—strategies that can stifle creativity and do not truly engage students. The workplace isn't stagnant; it's a lively space filled with constant changes and new ideas. Therefore, our education system needs to shift away from a one-size-fits-all approach to a more flexible framework that encourages creativity, critical thinking, and tech skills. Only then can we truly prepare our workforce for the challenges on the horizon.

Let's consider creativity in education. It's concerning how often creativity gets pushed aside in favor of traditional subjects. Yes, math and science are crucial, but the ability to think creatively and solve problems is becoming increasingly important in today's job market. Employers want more than just workers who can complete tasks; they're looking for people who can innovate and bring fresh ideas to the table. A curriculum that fosters creativity will help students confidently tackle complex problems with imagination and skill.

We also need to focus more on problem-solving skills in our schools. Many students graduate with a lot of theoretical knowledge, but they often struggle to apply that knowledge in real-world situations. We need to nurture a generation of thinkers who can assess problems, brainstorm solutions, and put those solutions into action. This means schools need to offer hands-on learning experiences that promote exploration and experimentation. By rethinking our approach to education, we can equip students with the skills they need to navigate the uncertainties of today's job market.

Additionally, technological literacy has become a must-have skill. Technology influences nearly every part of our lives—from how we communicate to how we manage our health and finances. Understanding how to use these tools effectively is critical. Schools need to weave technology into their learning programs, treating it as a core part of education rather than an afterthought. This involves teaching students not only how to use technology responsibly and creatively but also how to think critically about it. We want to cultivate not just consumers of technology but also innovators who can push boundaries.

Looking ahead, we envision a future where collaboration between schools and tech companies is standard practice. Such partnerships can help create a curriculum that meets the evolving needs of employers, ensuring that students learn the skills that are truly in demand. Imagine if tech companies worked hand-in-hand with schools to shape educational programs, offer internships, and provide mentoring. This kind of collaboration would enrich students' learning experiences while also developing a pipeline of skilled workers ready to step into the workforce.

Successful education programs that prioritize hands-on learning give us a glimpse into this exciting future. For example, programs that incorporate internships into students' studies allow them to gain real-world experience while still in school. This not only helps them build their resumes but also gives them a clearer picture of what employers are looking for. Mentorship programs can significantly impact students' career paths, offering guidance, networking opportunities, and inspiration from professionals in their desired fields.

Take coding boot camps as an example. These programs, often run in partnership with tech companies, provide fast-paced and focused training to help individuals gain the coding skills necessary for today's digital jobs. These initiatives clearly show how educational reform can happen beyond traditional classrooms, offering the flexibility needed to keep up with a fast-moving job market.

Also, we shouldn't forget about the importance of lifelong learning in this new landscape. The days of finishing school and thinking your education is done are long gone.

Ongoing professional development is key to career success now. As technology evolves at lightning speed, people need to adopt a mindset of lifelong learning, consistently seeking opportunities to update their skills and knowledge. Online courses, workshops, and certification programs are readily available, offering individuals ways to take charge of their learning paths.

In a world where change is the only constant, nurturing a culture of continuous learning will empower individuals to stay adaptable in their careers. This shift needs support not just from educational institutions, but also from employers. Companies that invest in their employees' growth foster a more engaged and skilled workforce. When workers feel valued and see opportunities for advancement, they are more likely to contribute positively to their organizations.

As we picture this empowered workforce, we must recognize the role of supportive policies and practices in driving educational reform and lifelong learning. Governments and educational leaders should prioritize funding for innovative programs that connect education to employment. This includes investing in professional development for educators to keep them updated on the latest teaching strategies that engage students. Policymakers should also push for flexibility within the education system, allowing schools to adapt their curricula in response to the needs of the job market.

The conversation about education needs to broaden beyond just academic achievement to include a focus on skills, creativity, and adaptability. Educational reform is not simply about updating curricula; it's about rethinking education's purpose within a tech-driven economy. We should view education not just as a ticket to a job but as a lifelong journey of growth and exploration.

As we stand at this pivotal moment, we have the chance to create a future where work is not just about getting by but about fulfilling our potential and advancing society as a whole. The aim is not just to get individuals jobs, but to cultivate a workforce that is empowered, flexible, and ready to thrive in a changing world. By supporting educational reform and promoting a culture of lifelong learning, we can spark a movement toward a more inclusive future—where everyone has the chance to make meaningful contributions to society and reach their fullest potential.

The future of work is bright, but it will take a collective effort to make it happen. By advocating for innovative education and lifelong learning opportunities, we can mold a generation of thinkers, creators, and leaders who will not only meet the challenges of a tech-driven economy but also redefine what work can be. The road ahead is full of promise, and as we empower the workforce of tomorrow, we're not just preparing for what's to come; we're actively shaping it. Together, let's embrace the opportunities before us and strive for a future that puts purpose, innovation, and progress at the heart of our shared goals.

Cornel Jefferson

Chapter 8: Technological Solutions to Global Challenges

Conquering Climate Change

The world is standing on the edge, with the threats of climate change becoming more evident each year. The signs are clear: glaciers are melting quicker than it takes to make a cup of coffee, wildfires rage as if the planet is expressing its frustration, and storms are becoming more severe, demonstrating nature's wrath. Yet, despite these overwhelming challenges, there's a bright side: technology, both a challenge and an opportunity in our time, offers not just a chance for survival but also a spark for fresh ideas and actions that can tackle this crisis effectively.

Now more than ever, we need sustainable solutions. The advancements in renewable energy technologies signal a new age of possibilities. Picture a world where the sun's energy, captured through extensive solar panels, powers our homes, schools, and businesses. Imagine wind turbines swaying gently in the breeze, turning the power of the wind into the electricity that brightens our lives. Think about hydroelectric systems harnessing the steady flow of rivers to produce clean energy while protecting the thriving ecosystems around them. These technologies aren't just dreams for tomorrow; they're already being developed and used around the world, showing how human creativity can rise to meet the urgent challenges we face.

Solar energy is perhaps the most noticeable player in this ongoing story. With the price of solar panels dropping significantly in recent years, households and businesses are eagerly adopting this technology. Solar energy isn't just a passing trend; it's a movement that pushes us toward energy independence. Homes equipped with solar panels are not only shrinking their carbon footprints but also taking charge of their own electricity generation. This shift is both good for the environment and beneficial for the economy. Consequently, the solar industry is booming, creating jobs in manufacturing, installation, and maintenance.

While solar energy shines brightly, wind power is also making a significant impact on the global energy scene. Wind farms, stretching across plains and coastlines, have become familiar sights. The technology behind wind energy has improved, with larger turbines and better materials enhancing efficiency and output. When these windmills turn, they generate not just electricity but also hope for a cleaner, greener future. Countries like Denmark and Spain have successfully woven wind energy into their national electricity grids, proving that transitioning to renewable sources can be both practical and transformative. Plus, advancements in energy storage, like improved battery systems, are making it possible to capture wind energy even when the wind isn't blowing.

However, renewable energy is just part of the solution. The rise of smart grid technology is another major advancement in the fight against climate change. Smart grids—systems that allow for real-time monitoring and management of electricity flow—are changing how we use and share energy. Imagine a world where your thermostat adjusts based on energy prices, where electric vehicles charge during low-demand hours, and where communities share energy resources effortlessly. This kind of interconnectedness creates a stronger and more efficient energy system, reducing waste and maximizing the use of renewable resources. Smart grids not only empower consumers; they also pave the way for a future where local energy production and consumption thrive, ultimately decreasing our dependence on fossil fuels.

The potential of technology goes beyond just renewable energy. Innovations in carbon capture and storage (CCS) are becoming crucial in the battle against climate change. These technologies capture carbon dioxide emissions from places like power plants and factories, preventing them from entering the atmosphere. Once captured, this CO_2 can be used in products such as concrete or stored deep underground, effectively removing it from the carbon cycle. Although still in its early stages, CCS offers a promising glimpse into a future where industries can continue operating while greatly reducing their environmental impact. The challenge is to scale up these technologies so they can make a real difference, but with ongoing investment and innovation, CCS could be key in reaching net-zero emissions.

Moreover, technology's role in fighting climate change goes beyond energy production. New approaches in agriculture, like precision farming and vertical farming, could transform how we grow our food. By using satellite imagery, drones, and advanced sensors, farmers can monitor their crops in real-time, optimizing their use of resources and cutting down on waste. This precision boosts yields and minimizes the environmental harm often associated with traditional farming, which has long relied on pesticides and fertilizers. Vertical farming, which allows food to be grown in urban settings, promotes local production, reducing transportation emissions and providing fresh produce in areas that lack access.

As we consider these technological solutions, it's crucial to remember that progress doesn't happen in isolation. It requires supportive policies, investment, and a culture that welcomes change. Governments around the world need to focus on research and development in renewable energy and other climate-friendly technologies. Collaborations between public and private sectors can drive advancements by combining resources and expertise. Notably, the investment landscape is evolving, with more venture capitalists looking to fund startups focused on climate solutions. This influx of capital is fostering innovation at a speed that is both exciting and necessary.

Additionally, the power of grassroots movements should not be overlooked. People across the globe are calling for action from their leaders, pushing for policies that promote sustainability and environmental care. The urgency behind these movements reflects a growing understanding that the stakes are high. Climate change isn't a distant issue; it's a pressing crisis that needs everyone's involvement. Technology is a critical piece of the puzzle, but we need collective efforts from all corners of society—individuals, businesses, and governments alike.

Education is a key element in this push for collective action. By giving people the knowledge and skills to understand and engage with climate technologies, we can inspire a new generation of changemakers. Schools and universities should prioritize sustainability in their teachings, emphasizing the importance of innovation and environmental responsibility. These future leaders will be better equipped to advocate for and implement the technological solutions that will shape the next wave of climate action.

While the path ahead is filled with obstacles, the promise of technology to combat climate change fills us with hope. The blend of innovation and determination has the potential to change our planet's future for the better. Humanity's ability to create and solve problems knows no bounds. By using the tools we have, we can find a way to a sustainable and thriving world. This journey will demand steadfast commitment, cooperation, and a shared vision, but the benefits—clean air, plentiful resources, and a stable climate—make it all worthwhile. The time to act is now, and the solutions are within our reach. Together, we can turn the tide against climate change, ensuring a healthier planet for generations to come.

Eradicating Scarcity

Poverty and resource scarcity aren't just cold statistics; they are real struggles that affect billions of people around the world. Each number related to hunger or the lack of clean water tells the story of individuals with dreams, hardships, and a yearning for a better life. These challenges are deeply connected to our society, influencing everything from health and education to economic stability and community bonds. But amidst the challenges, there is hope. Technology shines brightly as a source of potential, offering creative solutions that can significantly change these tough circumstances.

At the heart of tackling scarcity is the urgent issue of food security, which has become more critical as the global population keeps rising. According to the United Nations, by

2050, the world's population could hit an astonishing 9.7 billion. This growth means we need to rethink how we farm so that we can feed everyone without harming our already stressed planet. Here's where agricultural innovations come into play—technologies like vertical farming, precision agriculture, and genetically modified organisms (GMOs) are leading the way in transforming our farming practices. These advancements not only aim to boost food production but also do so with a focus on reducing environmental harm, paving the way for a sustainable future.

Vertical farming is an exciting innovation that literally takes food production to new heights. Picture a tall building filled with many layers of crops, all grown indoors using hydroponics or aeroponics. This method allows for year-round growth, unaffected by weather or seasonal changes. It drastically cuts down the land needed for farming and lowers transportation costs and emissions by allowing food to be grown in cities, where demand is highest. Plus, using LED lights specifically designed for plant growth makes this method even more efficient, allowing crops to thrive in conditions that used to be impossible.

Alongside vertical farming, precision agriculture is transforming how farmers care for their land. With tools like satellite images, drones, and advanced sensors, farmers can collect real-time information about their crops and soil. This technology enables them to water, fertilize, or use pesticides only where necessary, cutting down on waste and protecting the environment. By using resources wisely, farmers can boost their yields while conserving water and using fewer harmful chemicals. This approach not only strengthens food security but also nurtures healthier ecosystems, making it beneficial for both people and the planet.

Genetically modified organisms (GMOs) can be a hot topic, but we can't ignore their potential to help with scarcity. By changing the genetic structure of crops, scientists can make them more resistant to pests, diseases, and tough environmental conditions like drought or poor soil. These tweaks can lead to higher yields and allow crops to be grown in places that were once thought too harsh for farming. While the discussions around GMOs continue, it's important to look at how they can help tackle food scarcity, especially as climate change creates new challenges for traditional farming.

While agricultural technology plays a crucial role in fighting scarcity, having access to clean water is just as important. Water scarcity affects more than just farming; it also impacts health, education, and economic stability. As we look at innovations in water purification, we find exciting developments that could change the game for access to clean water, particularly in areas that need it most.

For example, membrane filtration technologies use semi-permeable membranes to filter out contaminants from water. This method is not only effective but can be scaled for different needs, from small home systems to large city plants. These technologies can offer a dependable source of clean water, significantly improving health and sanitation in places where safe drinking water is still a luxury.

Another encouraging method is solar water disinfection, which uses sunlight to purify water. By simply placing contaminated water in clear bottles and leaving them in the sun, harmful microorganisms can be effectively destroyed. This low-cost, sustainable solution is especially useful for rural communities lacking the necessary infrastructure. As we face the global water crisis, such innovations offer hope for a future where clean water is a basic right for everyone.

However, even with advancements in agriculture and water purification, we can't fully tackle scarcity without addressing how resources are shared. We need economic models that promote fair distribution to ensure that these technological breakthroughs reach those who need them the most. New technologies, like blockchain, can improve transparency and fairness in supply chains, helping to create systems that promote equal access to resources while reducing waste and corruption.

Blockchain technology, often linked with cryptocurrencies, provides a decentralized way of keeping records that can be used across different sectors, including farming and water distribution. By creating a secure record of transactions, blockchain can track how resources move from producers to consumers. This transparency helps ensure that farmers are paid fairly for their products and that resources are distributed efficiently. In areas struggling with corruption or inefficiency, such systems can promote fairness and empower local communities against scarcity.

Additionally, other innovative economic models are surfacing that focus on sustainability and social impact. Cooperative structures, for example, enable communities to pool resources and share responsibilities, often leading to greater efficiency and better results for everyone involved. By promoting teamwork instead of competition, these models can create a more inclusive way to share resources, tackling some of the root causes of poverty and scarcity.

As we consider these technological advancements and economic models, it's crucial to remember that they can't work in isolation. Successfully addressing scarcity needs a comprehensive approach that combines technology, policy, and grassroots efforts. Governments play a key role in shaping policies that support innovation, investment, and sustainable practices. By focusing on research and development in farming and water purification, leaders can create an environment where technology can thrive and help alleviate scarcity.

But policies alone aren't enough. Public awareness and community involvement are vital in driving the change we want to see. Grassroots movements around the world are speaking up, advocating for sustainable practices, and pushing for policies that prioritize the needs of those most affected. These movements highlight the understanding that scarcity isn't just an economic issue; it's a social crisis that demands urgent action from all parts of society.

Education is also a key player in the fight against scarcity. By giving individuals the knowledge and skills to engage with these technological solutions, we can inspire a new wave of changemakers. Schools and universities should prioritize sustainability and innovation in their programs, creating an environment where young people can imagine and develop the solutions of the future.

The journey to eliminate scarcity is undeniably complex, filled with challenges that might feel overwhelming. Yet, the ability of technology to change lives is incredibly powerful and full of promise. Every innovation, from vertical farms to water purification systems, is a step toward a world where scarcity is a thing of the past. By combining these advancements with fair economic models, we can build a future where everyone has access to the resources they need to thrive.

Ultimately, the effort to eradicate scarcity is a shared responsibility. It calls for teamwork among individuals, businesses, governments, and organizations working together to harness the potential of technology. By focusing on sustainability and fairness, we can open the doors to a brighter future—one where the burden of scarcity is lifted, and the possibility for prosperity shines brightly for everyone. We have the chance to create a world where hunger, lack of clean water, and economic inequality are no longer defining features of our global landscape. The time for action is now, and the solutions are right in front of us, ready to be embraced. Together, through innovation, commitment, and collaboration, we can make a significant impact against scarcity and build a future filled with hope and abundance.

Enhancing Quality of Life

The quality of life we enjoy is deeply influenced by the healthcare systems around us. There's a strong link between our health and the progress we've made in medical technology. Throughout history, healthcare innovations have completely changed our lives, turning once-fatal diseases into manageable conditions and increasing life expectancy. However, this journey hasn't always been easy, and we still face gaps in access to care. Today, we are in a unique position to use technology to improve healthcare—making it easier, more efficient, and effective for everyone.

Imagine a world where healthcare isn't just a luxury for a select few, but a fundamental right for all. Visualize a patient in a remote village being able to consult with a specialist from thousands of miles away, all thanks to telemedicine. Think about artificial intelligence being able to diagnose health issues with incredible precision, allowing doctors to spend more time caring for their patients. Picture breakthroughs in biotechnology that create treatment plans tailored specifically to each person's genetic profile. These aren't just dreams; they are happening now, reshaping healthcare and bringing hope for a healthier future for everyone.

Telemedicine is leading this change, breaking down the barriers that often make healthcare hard to access, especially for those in rural or low-income areas. With just a smartphone or computer, patients can have video calls with doctors for advice, prescriptions, and follow-ups—all from the comfort of their own homes. This is more than just a convenience; it's a vital resource for those who struggle to get to traditional healthcare facilities. A study in the American Journal of Managed Care found that telehealth visits surged by 154% in the early months of the pandemic, highlighting how virtual healthcare can meet urgent needs.

Telemedicine also has a significant impact on mental health, a crucial aspect of our overall well-being that often gets overlooked. Remote sessions with mental health professionals help to erase the stigma around asking for help and provide a safe space for people to discuss their challenges. With platforms like BetterHelp and Talkspace, individuals now have access to therapy that fits their schedules and preferences. The option to seek mental health support without the stress of visiting a clinic can greatly improve quality of life for many.

The rise of artificial intelligence in healthcare is set to change patient care and diagnostics for the better. AI tools are being created to sift through huge amounts of medical data, spotting trends and making predictions that a human might miss. For example, AI can now analyze medical images—like X-rays and MRIs—with remarkable accuracy, often doing a better job than human radiologists at finding problems. This technology can lead to earlier diagnoses, which is critical for diseases like cancer, where catching it early can dramatically boost survival rates.

Additionally, AI has a big role to play in personalized medicine, where treatments are customized to fit each patient's unique needs. By looking at genetic information, lifestyle choices, and environmental factors, AI can guide doctors in choosing the most effective treatment for every individual. This approach moves away from the one-size-fits-all model to a more tailored strategy that considers each patient's specific circumstances. The promise of personalized medicine lies not just in better treatment outcomes, but also in reducing side effects that generic treatments might cause.

Biotechnology is another exciting area where technology can greatly improve our lives. From gene-editing techniques like CRISPR to new drug development, biotechnology is creating innovative answers to long-standing health challenges. Gene therapy, for instance, could treat genetic disorders by fixing the faulty genes that cause them. This groundbreaking method holds the potential to wipe out diseases that have troubled us for generations, including inherited conditions once thought to be untreatable.

Moreover, progress in biotechnology is leading to developments in regenerative medicine, which uses stem cells to repair or replace damaged tissues and organs. Imagine a future where spinal cord injuries no longer result in permanent paralysis or where damaged hearts can heal themselves. This isn't just a fantasy; it is on the horizon and could completely change how we approach healthcare, improving quality of life for countless people.

However, despite the incredible potential of these technologies, we need to be mindful of the challenges they bring. Access to care and equity are critical issues that we must address. Rapid advancements often mean that people in lower-income or rural areas might miss out on the latest treatments available in cities. Telemedicine, for example, relies on reliable internet access, which isn't available everywhere. If we're not careful, these gaps in healthcare can widen, leading to even greater health disparities.

To tackle these challenges, it's vital for governments, organizations, and communities to join forces to ensure that everyone can benefit from advancements in healthcare technology. Policymakers should focus on improving digital infrastructure, especially in underserved areas, to make telemedicine and digital health resources more available. Partnerships between tech companies and healthcare providers can help create solutions that meet the specific needs of disadvantaged communities, so no one is left behind.

Education also plays a key role in improving quality of life through healthcare technology. Training healthcare professionals to use new technologies effectively allows them to maximize their benefits. At the same time, informing patients about their options gives them the power to take control of their health. When patients understand how technology can help them, they become active participants in their care rather than just passive recipients.

Healthcare literacy is essential in a world where patients are more empowered to make informed choices about their treatment. Workshops, community programs, and online resources can help close the knowledge gap, giving individuals the confidence to navigate the complexities of healthcare technology. This shift toward patient-centered care highlights how important communication and collaboration between providers and patients are, contributing to a healthier society.

Looking ahead, we also need to think about the ethical questions surrounding the technologies we adopt. With great advancements come great responsibilities, and as we integrate AI and biotechnology into healthcare, we must address concerns about data privacy, consent, and possible biases in machine learning systems. Creating ethical guidelines is crucial to ensure these technologies benefit everyone and don't deepen existing inequalities.

It's essential for the medical community, along with technologists, ethicists, and legislators, to have ongoing conversations about these issues and create standards that prioritize patient safety and fairness. The aim should be to foster an environment where technology improves quality of life without compromising ethical standards or human dignity.

Overall, the relationship between technology and healthcare is one of the most exciting stories of our time. As we use innovative solutions to tackle the health challenges we face today, we must stay committed to accessibility, equity, and ethical considerations. Together, we can create a healthcare system where technological advancements go hand in hand with compassion and understanding, moving us toward a future where quality of life is a reality for everyone.

 The journey to improve quality of life through technology in healthcare is about more than just new tools; it's about nurturing a spirit of hope and resilience. It's about rethinking what's possible and working together to build a world where each person can lead a healthy, fulfilling life. By embracing technology's potential while staying grounded in our shared humanity, we can truly change the healthcare landscape, making the promise of a better future attainable for all.

Cornel Jefferson

Chapter 9: Fostering a Pro-Progress Culture

Mindset Shift: Cultivating a Culture of Optimism and Innovation

In our tech-driven world, the stories we tell about the future have a huge impact. They shape how people, companies, and even whole communities react to the fast changes happening around us. Often, the conversation about technology leans toward fear—talking about job loss, ethical issues, and even threats to our existence. But there's another way to look at things, one that focuses on hope and creativity. This perspective aims to turn fear into excitement, uncertainty into opportunities, and stagnation into progress.

Imagine a world where technology isn't seen as a danger but as a powerful tool for empowerment. This shift in thinking isn't just a nice idea; it's crucial for thriving in a constantly changing environment. When communities embrace a culture of optimism, they can tap into technology's potential, leading to solutions that improve lives and drive progress. So, how do we spark this passion for innovation and possibility?

At the core of this cultural change is an important insight: our mindset can be changed. It's like clay that can be shaped and reshaped in the hands of a skilled artist. Leaders, teachers, and visionaries play a key role in guiding this shift. They need to advocate for positive change while also living it out in their actions. This means creating spaces where curiosity is cherished, experimentation is welcomed, and failures are seen as stepping stones on the path to success.

One of the most effective ways to nurture a culture of optimism is through storytelling. Stories connect with our hearts and minds, casting technology as the hero in our shared journey rather than the villain. Take the internet as an example: it started as a military project meant for communication among defense contractors. Now, it's vital for global connection, helping everything from social movements to telehealth. By sharing stories of innovation that have made a difference, we inspire people to imagine what's possible instead of worrying about what might go wrong.

Changing our mindset also means tackling the fears that often come with new technology. Look at the rise of artificial intelligence, for instance. Many people think of AI as a threat, bringing job losses and a bleak future. But AI is also being used in many ways to help solve big problems—like improving healthcare and understanding climate change. By changing the way we talk about technology, we can shift the focus from fear to excitement about the possibilities ahead.

Organizations can also create a culture of innovation by encouraging a spirit of experimentation. For example, Google is famous for its "20% time" policy, allowing employees to spend part of their workweek on passion projects. This not only leads to groundbreaking products but also makes employees feel more engaged and invested in their work. When people feel empowered to pursue their ideas, they're more likely to contribute creatively and collaboratively, opening doors to innovation that might have otherwise stayed shut.

Leaders play a crucial role in this cultural shift. They need to demonstrate the values of optimism and innovation by creating an environment where team members feel safe to take risks and share their ideas. This involves having emotional intelligence, which means being aware of and addressing their team's fears and concerns. By listening actively and acknowledging their worries, leaders can build trust, paving the way for open conversations and teamwork.

Moreover, leaders should prioritize transparency within their organizations. When people understand the reasons behind decisions and the bigger picture, they're more likely to feel invested in what happens next. Transparency creates a sense of belonging where everyone feels their opinion counts. This shared engagement is vital for fostering a mindset that welcomes innovation and growth.

The move towards a culture that encourages progress benefits not just organizations but also individuals. A culture that values experimentation, embraces failures, and celebrates innovation empowers people to chase their passions and make meaningful contributions to society. When individuals feel hopeful about their ability to make a difference, they're more likely to take initiative, work together, and support one another in their efforts.

Educational institutions also play a key role in shaping this culture of optimism. By teaching students a growth mindset—the idea that intelligence and skills can be developed through effort and determination—schools can prepare young people to embrace innovation instead of fearing it. Encouraging hands-on learning, where students tackle real-world issues with creative solutions, helps them feel capable and empowers them to see challenges as opportunities.

Additionally, communities can boost a culture of optimism by creating spaces for collaboration and discussion. Think tanks, innovation hubs, and co-working spaces offer a great environment for sharing ideas and solving problems together. These places break down barriers and bring together different viewpoints, sparking creativity in ways that working in isolation cannot achieve.

As we reflect on the role of technology in our lives, it's vital to remember that it mirrors our shared values and dreams. When we embrace a culture that celebrates innovation, we open the door to advancements that not only drive economic growth but also improve our quality of life. This shift goes beyond just adopting new technologies; it's about rethinking our relationship with them.

In many ways, the technology we develop is a reflection of our hopefulness. The breakthroughs we see in areas like renewable energy, healthcare, and education showcase the power of human creativity and teamwork. By fostering a culture that prioritizes innovation, we empower ourselves to address the pressing challenges facing our society, such as climate change and social inequality.

Creating a culture of optimism and innovation requires intention and dedication. It calls for us to work together to change mindsets, celebrate creativity, and embrace uncertainty. As we take part in this transformative journey, we should remember that the future isn't set in stone; it's a canvas for us to paint our shared dreams upon.

As we move forward, let's aim to build a world where technology is seen as a force for good, where innovation is part of our everyday lives, and where optimism leads the way. In this world, individuals and communities will flourish, empowered to reach their full potential and shape a future filled with hope and possibilities.

Through a culture of optimism and innovation, we can navigate today's complexities, using technology to create a lasting impact for future generations. The road may have its bumps, but the benefits of fostering a culture that embraces progress far outweigh the challenges. It's time for us to shift our mindset, welcome innovation, and prepare for a brighter future overflowing with opportunities. After all, the greatest achievements often bloom from the seeds of hope sown in the rich soil of possibility.

Overcoming Fear and Doubt: Addressing Concerns about Technological Advancement

In today's fast-changing digital world, worries about technology are just as common as the innovations themselves. It's easy to see why many people feel anxious about automation, artificial intelligence, and other new technologies. Concerns about losing jobs, ethical questions surrounding AI, and growing social inequalities fueled by tech are heavy on many minds. As we face these advancements, it's clear that these fears come from genuine worries about what the future holds for us all.

Let's consider the anxiety tied to job loss. The narrative often paints a bleak picture: machines will take over, leaving countless workers without jobs and struggling to survive. In various sectors, from manufacturing to customer service, automation is already reshaping traditional roles—sometimes at a startling pace. But could we approach this shift with proactive strategies that ease fears and create fresh opportunities? The key is to embrace open discussions, smart policy-making, and share success stories that show how communities can adapt to these changes.

Open discussions are vital for tackling the worries that come with tech advancements. By creating spaces where people from different walks of life can gather, we can foster a culture of openness. These forums allow individuals to express their fears while also learning from experts who can help clarify the technology landscape. When we include voices from affected workers, tech developers, ethicists, and community leaders, we can deepen our understanding of the challenges and opportunities technology brings. The goal is to create conversations that welcome tough questions and seek collaborative solutions.

Imagine a town hall meeting where a community is faced with the possibility of an automated factory moving in. The tension is palpable—what will happen to the jobs that have supported families for years? Yet, by bringing together workers, business leaders, and tech experts, the dialogue can switch from fear to empowerment. Together, they can brainstorm retraining programs to prepare the workforce for new positions, ensuring no one gets left behind as industries change. This kind of teamwork is crucial for building a sense of community ownership over the transformations happening around them.

Policy development is another crucial way to tackle concerns about tech advancements. It's important to push for policies that protect us from the negative effects of automation and AI while also encouraging innovation. One promising idea gaining ground is universal basic income (UBI), which could provide a financial safety net for those affected by job loss. By giving individuals a stable financial foundation, UBI would allow workers to pursue education, start businesses, or retrain for new careers without the immediate worry of financial strain.

Retraining programs play a key role too, helping workers shift into new job markets. The job landscape is changing rapidly; many positions that are common today may not exist in the next decade. By investing in training initiatives that focus on skills relevant to our tech-driven economy, we can prepare the workforce for the future and ease fears about job loss. The challenge is to make sure these programs are accessible to everyone, ensuring that marginalized communities aren't left behind.

Success stories can shine a light of hope amid all this uncertainty. Many communities and organizations have effectively adapted to technological disruptions by welcoming change instead of resisting it. Consider a small town that faced the closure of a manufacturing plant due to automation. Rather than giving in to despair, the community united to seek out new opportunities. They initiated retraining programs that provided workers with digital skills, allowing them to transition into tech-related jobs. As a result, not only did the town keep its workforce, but it also attracted new businesses eager to tap into the skilled labor pool created by these efforts.

Sharing these success stories can inspire others facing similar challenges. They highlight the potential for positive change and show that fear can be a powerful motivator for action. When communities see real examples of resilience and innovation, it can spark hope and encourage individuals to engage more actively with the technological world around them. The strength of these stories is that they make the challenges of technological change relatable, illustrating that while the road ahead may be tough, it is also filled with chances for growth and reinvention.

 When channeled positively, fear can drive us toward meaningful changes. It can ignite curiosity, prompting people to seek information and resources that empower them to adapt to new realities. By proactively engaging with technology instead of retreating into doubt, we can create an environment ripe for innovation and progress. This calls for all of us to work together—a commitment to building a culture where open conversations, collaboration, and smart policy-making are at the forefront.

 Additionally, it's crucial for leaders in all sectors to champion these efforts. They should represent the values of hope and teamwork, leading by example in their commitment to engaging communities in meaningful discussions about the impacts of technology. When leaders advocate for open dialogues and support policy development, they help build trust and transparency, encouraging individuals to share their concerns and hopes.

 As we navigate the realities of technological advancement, let's remember that our fears, while valid, don't have to hold us back. Instead, they can inspire us to take action—a call for individuals, communities, and policymakers to come together. By embracing open conversations, crafting thoughtful policies, and celebrating success stories, we can tackle the complexities of technological change as a unified front.

Ultimately, the future isn't set in stone; it's a blank canvas, waiting for us to paint our dreams on. Through open discussions, proactive policy-making, and a focus on uplifting stories, we can turn fear into action, skepticism into engagement, and uncertainty into opportunity. The path ahead may be challenging, but by confronting our fears and doubts, we can welcome a future where technology improves our lives and strengthens our communities. Together, we hold the power to shape the narrative of technological advancement, ensuring it becomes a force for good rather than a source of worry.

Inspiring the Next Generation: Nurturing Future Innovators and Thinkers

At the heart of any vibrant society is the ability to inspire and nurture the next generation. This crucial task goes far beyond simply passing down knowledge; it involves fostering creativity, critical thinking, and a deep curiosity about the world around us. As technology continues to advance at lightning speed, nurturing our youth becomes even more essential. Education and mentorship play key roles in this effort, acting as the sturdy pillars that will support tomorrow's innovators, thinkers, and creators as they navigate the complexities ahead.

When we think about changing our educational systems, it's clear that we need to rethink the old ways of teaching. The traditional approach, which often focuses on memorization and standardized tests, doesn't really prepare students for a world that values adaptability and innovative problem-solving. Instead, we should create curricula that blend STEM (Science, Technology, Engineering, and Mathematics) with the arts and humanities. This balanced approach nurtures well-rounded individuals who can draw from a variety of knowledge areas, enhancing their ability to innovate and think critically.

To really grasp the need for this new direction, picture a classroom where students aren't just sitting quietly, absorbing information. Imagine a lively space filled with hands-on projects where they apply scientific ideas to real-life problems. For example, rather than just reading about physics in textbooks, students could design and build their own roller coasters using engineering and physics concepts. They wouldn't just learn about forces, energy, and motion; they'd experience the excitement of watching their designs come to life. Such active learning sparks a love for discovery and encourages students to push the limits of their imagination.

A crucial part of this educational shift is bringing technology into learning. Technology isn't just another tool; it opens doors to incredible opportunities for exploration and creativity. Classrooms equipped with modern tech—like virtual reality, coding platforms, and robotics kits—can change the way students learn. They allow kids to dive into simulations, work with complex data, and collaborate on projects that go beyond borders. This kind of learning sets students up for careers in tech-focused industries, giving them a sense of control over their futures.

But having a thoughtful curriculum isn't enough on its own. The importance of mentorship is huge when it comes to guiding young minds. Pairing students with mentors who work in technology and related fields can offer them invaluable insights and a spark of inspiration. Mentorship programs open up paths for students to tackle real-world challenges, learn from seasoned professionals, and get support as they navigate their educational journeys. These connections can shape how students view their potential and help them discover opportunities that might have seemed out of reach.

    Take Maria, a young girl from a community where few people pursued careers in technology. Her high school had limited resources, and the common belief was that tech was meant for the privileged. However, through a local mentorship program, Maria was matched with a software engineer who saw her potential. This mentor introduced her to coding, encouraged her to join tech competitions, and helped her create a portfolio showcasing her work. Maria not only found her passion for technology; she also gained the confidence to apply for scholarships and ended up getting into a prestigious university's computer science program. Her story highlights how powerful mentorship can be, shining a light on paths that might have previously felt dark or unavailable.

    Furthermore, engaging the community is a vital part of nurturing future innovators. When communities come together to support initiatives that promote access to technology and innovation, they create spaces where young people can thrive. Events like hackathons, innovation labs, and tech fairs offer opportunities for youth to collaborate, experiment, and learn from each other. These hands-on experiences foster a sense of belonging and reinforce the idea that innovation isn't just for a select few; it's something everyone can pursue.

Imagine a local hackathon focused on solving community problems, like environmental sustainability or healthcare access. Young participants from various backgrounds come together to brainstorm, code, and pitch their ideas. Through this teamwork, they not only learn new technical skills but also develop empathy and a deeper understanding of their community's challenges. They become change-makers, empowered to use their knowledge and creativity to make a difference.

Such community initiatives also help level the playing field for underrepresented groups in technology. By actively promoting diversity and inclusion, we can ensure that every voice is heard and valued. This means tackling barriers that keep certain groups from accessing tech opportunities and actively involving marginalized communities. Programs aimed at girls, youth of color, and low-income students can help break the misconceptions that tech is exclusive or out of reach. By creating welcoming and supportive spaces for these individuals, we empower them to confidently pursue careers in STEM fields.

The urgency of nurturing the next generation cannot be ignored. The challenges we face—climate change, social inequality, and technological disruption—call for innovative solutions that come from fresh perspectives. By investing in the education and mentorship of young people, we are effectively laying the groundwork for a more equitable and sustainable future. Tomorrow's leaders are not just bystanders; they are active players in shaping the world around them. By giving them the tools, resources, and support they need, we enable them to realize their potential and contribute to a society that values creativity and progress.

Moreover, as we think about the importance of education, mentorship, and community involvement, we must acknowledge that this mission doesn't fall solely on the shoulders of educators or policymakers. It requires a collective effort from businesses, nonprofits, and civic organizations. The private sector has a unique chance to partner with schools and communities to create meaningful internships, sponsor educational initiatives, and back mentorship programs. By investing in the next generation, companies can help build a skilled workforce and demonstrate a commitment to corporate responsibility and community support.

The effects of fostering future innovators go far beyond the individual. As these young minds grow into leaders and changemakers, they will carry forward the values of innovation, collaboration, and compassion. They will challenge the status quo, push the limits of technology, and tackle the pressing issues we face today. In a world often marked by division and uncertainty, the potential for unity through shared purpose rests on the strength of the next generation.

As we look ahead, let's embrace the responsibility of nurturing young innovators with enthusiasm. Our collective investment in their education, mentorship, and community involvement will reap benefits that last for generations. By creating a culture that celebrates curiosity, creativity, and collaboration, we empower youth to dream big and chase their passions boldly. The future is not just a result of the past; it's shaped by the hopes and actions of those we choose to inspire today.

So, let's come together—parents, educators, mentors, community leaders, and advocates—to build a world where every child has access to the tools, opportunities, and support they need to explore their potential. This is our moment to ignite the flames of innovation and creativity in young minds, ensuring they're ready to face tomorrow's challenges with resilience, optimism, and purpose. In doing so, we elevate individuals and enrich the fabric of our society as a whole. The architects of our future are waiting for us to empower them, and it's our responsibility to ensure they're ready to build a world that reflects the best of humanity.

Cornel Jefferson

Chapter 10: Accelerating Towards a Limitless Future

The Roadmap Ahead: Practical Steps for Embracing Accelerationism

Embracing accelerationism means stepping into a world where we question the traditional norms of society and open ourselves up to endless possibilities for innovation. This isn't just an abstract idea; it's about taking real, practical steps that can change how individuals, organizations, and governments view progress and the future. It's about moving away from a mindset that gets stuck in stagnation and instead celebrating rapid growth and adaptability. The path ahead may be intricate, but it offers a chance for us to build a more prosperous, inventive, and fair society.

At the heart of this change is the development of an accelerationist mindset. This way of thinking is grounded in the belief that innovation is powerful and that failure isn't the end—it's a crucial part of the journey to success. It encourages people and organizations to prioritize trying out new things, to challenge the status quo, and to see every setback as a lesson rather than a reason to give up. By nurturing a culture that values these ideas, we can create an environment where creativity thrives, and fresh concepts can be explored without the fear of failure getting in the way of progress.

One of the best ways to foster innovation in organizations is to create dedicated teams and resources aimed at exploring new ideas. This could take shape as innovation labs, where diverse groups come together to brainstorm, prototype, and test exciting new concepts. A great example of this is Google's "20% time," where employees are allowed to spend part of their workweek on passion projects that aren't directly tied to their job roles. This approach has led to amazing products like Gmail and Google News, showing how prioritizing an innovative culture can yield incredible results.

Additionally, hosting hackathons can be a fantastic way to boost creativity and teamwork among employees. These high-energy events encourage teams to dive deep into a project over a short period, often leading to innovative solutions that wouldn't come up in a typical work setting. Organizations should actively support these collaborative efforts, as they not only spark fresh ideas but also strengthen team dynamics and increase employee satisfaction.

Building partnerships with startups can further enhance the innovation landscape for larger organizations. Startups usually operate with more agility and fewer bureaucratic obstacles than bigger companies, making them valuable allies in the quest for innovative solutions. By creating an environment where established companies and startups can share knowledge and resources, both sides can benefit, leading to groundbreaking advancements.

Another vital step in embracing accelerationism is understanding the array of technological tools at our disposal. In a world where decisions are often driven by data, organizations need to use technology to boost efficiency and improve interactions with customers. Tools that harness artificial intelligence to analyze consumer behavior can offer insights that help businesses tailor their products and services to meet the changing needs of their customers.

Moreover, software that facilitates smooth communication and project management can streamline workflows, allowing teams to collaborate more effectively, no matter where they are located. Tools like Slack or Asana have transformed how teams communicate, providing instant connectivity and accountability that enhances productivity. By incorporating these technologies into their operations, organizations can better respond to changes in the market and improve their overall performance.

Government policy is just as important in this accelerationist framework. Policymakers have the power to create flexible regulations that keep pace with the fast-moving world of technology. A key aspect of effective governance in this context is recognizing and revising outdated rules that may stifle innovation. For instance, some data privacy laws might need to be updated to allow for the smooth sharing of information that's essential for successful technological integration.

Creating incentives for organizations that adopt accelerationist practices can also help drive this movement. Offering tax breaks for companies investing in research and development or grants for startups leading the way in innovative technologies can foster an environment where innovation can thrive. By rewarding companies that commit to adapting and evolving, governments can stimulate both economic growth and societal progress.

Moreover, engaging the community is a key piece of this plan for embracing accelerationism. Grassroots movements can serve as powerful agents for change, demonstrating how individuals can come together to influence national narratives and drive innovation from the ground up. Local initiatives can motivate citizens to take ownership of their accelerationist journeys, promoting collaboration and innovation within their communities.

Creating platforms for citizen involvement, such as community forums or collaborative projects, gives people a chance to share their ideas and concerns while actively shaping their surroundings. Educational programs that promote digital literacy and critical thinking equip citizens with the tools they need to engage meaningfully in a complex world of technology and innovation. By encouraging grassroots participation, communities can carve their paths toward acceleration and inspire wider movements that resonate at national or global levels.

The journey toward embracing accelerationism is filled with chances for innovation, collaboration, and community engagement. By fostering a culture that values experimentation and adaptability, individuals and organizations can thrive in an ever-changing world. Governments also have a crucial role in supporting this journey with policies that empower businesses and citizens to explore the endless potential of technology.

This isn't just a call to action—it's an invitation to join a movement aimed at transforming our societies for the better. The urgency of this effort is clear. As we face significant challenges like climate change, economic inequality, and social justice, the need for innovative solutions has never been more pressing. By embracing the principles of accelerationism together, we can tap into the power of technology and human creativity to create a brighter future for everyone.

While the road ahead may have its challenges, by following this roadmap and committing to these principles, each of us can make a meaningful contribution to the cause of effective accelerationism. The vision of a better world isn't just a distant dream; it's within our reach, waiting for us to take action and drive the change we want to see.

As we look forward to an exciting future, let's hold onto the vision of a society that values innovation, embraces change, and seeks to uplift every individual. The journey may be complex, but the rewards of collective action, creativity, and collaboration are truly limitless. Together, through our shared commitment to these ideals, we can move toward a future filled with promise and well-being for all.

Measuring Success: Indicators for Tracking Progress Toward a Better Future

As we approach a new era filled with exciting technological changes and shifts in our society, the need for effective ways to measure our progress is crystal clear. It's not enough just to say we want a future filled with innovation and growth; we need the right tools to figure out how we're doing and where we can improve. What will help us navigate the unknown? What signs will show us that we're truly moving toward a fairer and more prosperous society?

For a long time, we've relied on economic indicators as the main way to assess how well nations are doing. Standard measures like GDP growth, employment rates, and new business creation have shaped our understanding of prosperity. However, as we move into a world that's more interconnected and driven by technology, it's clear these indicators don't tell the whole story. They often overlook the complexities of human experiences and the inequalities that persist in our communities. We must consider the growing gap in income and access to technology, which can prevent whole neighborhoods from participating in the bright future we're aiming for.

To truly grasp what success means, we need to expand our view of prosperity. It's important to include factors that reflect not just economic strength but also social well-being and overall quality of life. Metrics that look at income distribution, access to crucial services, and technology availability can give us a fuller picture of how people and communities are faring as everything changes. For instance, the Gini coefficient, which measures income inequality, can reveal if economic growth is helping everyone or just benefiting a privileged few. By adopting a well-rounded approach to economic indicators, we can build a fairer system for judging our progress.

But economic indicators only tell part of the story. Social metrics are vital for capturing what it really means to thrive as a community. As we dive deeper into this fast-paced era, we can't forget that human experience is just as important as numbers. Happiness scores and community well-being surveys can help us understand how people are feeling during these times of change. These measures let us assess not only material conditions but also the emotional and mental health of our communities. We must strive to include the diverse experiences that shape our society in our measurements. The spirit of a community can't just be reflected in numbers; it also includes the rich stories of the people living there.

Take the World Happiness Report, for example. It ranks countries based on how happy their citizens say they are. While it might seem a bit abstract, the data shows real connections between well-being and social policies, highlighting how our societal choices can impact individual happiness. The insights gained from such studies can help decision-makers craft better policies that prioritize the health and happiness of everyone. By integrating these qualitative measures into our broader success framework, we can create a more vibrant and harmonious society.

In the realm of technology, having the right indicators is even more crucial. The speed of technological change can be overwhelming, and measuring progress in this area is key to understanding how well our society is embracing new advancements. Metrics that track how quickly new technologies are adopted, how much is invested in research and development, and the level of digital literacy can serve as signs of a community's readiness to engage with rapid change.

For instance, the increase in broadband internet access can show how well a society is connecting to new information and opportunities. High digital literacy rates indicate that people are prepared to use technology in meaningful ways, while strong investment in research and development reflects a commitment to innovation and future growth. Together, these indicators provide valuable insights into how well a society is navigating the complexities of an accelerating world.

But collecting data is just the start. Establishing effective feedback loops is crucial for continuous improvement and adaptability. To stay flexible and responsive, we need to take an iterative approach, where strategies and policies can be fine-tuned based on real-time insights. Regularly checking on our progress, coupled with open lines for public input, creates an environment where innovation can thrive.

Imagine a city rolling out a new public transportation initiative to ease congestion and promote sustainability. By gathering data on ridership patterns, travel times, and user satisfaction, city planners can tweak routes, schedules, and services to better meet the community's needs. This ongoing process not only improves efficiency but also strengthens community involvement, allowing residents to feel a sense of ownership over the changes happening around them. By embracing such feedback mechanisms, we can adapt to an ever-changing landscape, ensuring our strategies stay relevant and effective.

Moreover, we must acknowledge that measuring success is a team effort. It requires collaboration between different sectors—government, businesses, and community organizations must come together to create a shared vision for progress. Each group brings its own insights and expertise, fostering a collective understanding of what success really means. This collaborative spirit is key to unlocking the full potential of our aspirations for the future.

Consider how public-private partnerships can drive technological innovation. When governments team up with tech companies, they can combine their strengths to develop policies that encourage growth while also protecting public interests. Additionally, involving community organizations in the policymaking process ensures that the voices of underrepresented groups are heard and taken into account. These partnerships aren't just helpful; they're essential.

As we move forward toward a future full of possibilities, we must commit to a well-rounded approach to measuring success. By broadening our use of diverse economic indicators, embracing qualitative social metrics, and keeping an eye on technological advancements, we can create an environment that not only thrives but also lifts up every member of society. The road ahead may have its challenges, but through thoughtful measurement, ongoing feedback, and collaborative efforts, we can find our way to a brighter tomorrow.

In this rapidly changing world, our shared well-being depends on our ability to track progress accurately. The indicators we choose to focus on will shape our understanding of success and, in turn, influence the policies and practices that guide our shared journey. So, it's up to us to select metrics that reflect our values and dreams. We should strive for a future that doesn't just celebrate economic growth but also champions social fairness, technological progress, and the overall enhancement of human experience.

As we look to the future, let's remember that the pursuit of a limitless tomorrow isn't just a distant ideal; it's a concrete goal that calls for action, reflection, and adjustment. By nurturing a culture of measurement, we can ensure that our journey into the future is grounded in genuine progress, equitable growth, and a deep commitment to the well-being of all. The path ahead is lit by the insights we gain along the way, guiding us toward a future where innovation knows no limits and everyone has the chance to thrive.

United in Vision: Building a Global Collective to Facilitate Acceleration

The world is at a crucial turning point, facing remarkable changes in technology and society that have the potential to transform our lives in ways we can hardly imagine. Yet, with all this promise comes the reality that we can't tackle these changes by ourselves. Our interconnected world is complex, and it calls for a united effort that goes beyond borders, industries, and cultural differences. It's becoming increasingly clear that we need to create a global community driven by a common vision for growth. This vision isn't just about harnessing innovation; it's also about making sure its benefits are shared fairly among all people.

    At the core of this movement is the power of collaboration among different sectors. When governments, businesses, NGOs, and local communities work together, the chances for groundbreaking progress increase significantly. History offers many examples of how teamwork can lead to transformative results. One shining example is the Global Fund to Fight AIDS, Tuberculosis, and Malaria. This initiative shows us that when governments join forces with the private sector and civil society, they can make remarkable strides in the fight against diseases that mainly affect underserved populations. By pooling their resources, expertise, and networks, these groups have saved millions of lives and built sustainable health systems that continue to benefit communities long after the initial efforts have ended.

To make partnerships effective, we need to prioritize transparency, respect, and accountability. It's crucial for everyone involved to recognize and appreciate the unique roles each party plays. Governments can offer policies and funding, while businesses can bring technological advancements and market insights. NGOs often have valuable local knowledge and understanding of community needs. By fostering an environment where diverse stakeholders can communicate openly, we can create a culture of shared ownership, allowing everyone to participate in the acceleration process.

The impact of global alliances is also significant. International organizations play a vital role in creating a connected world that supports conversation, knowledge sharing, and joint ventures. The United Nations has been a leader in promoting cooperation among nations to tackle pressing global issues for years. The Sustainable Development Goals (SDGs) illustrate how the UN has rallied member states, civil society, and businesses around a common agenda. By encouraging collaboration on problems like poverty reduction, gender equality, and climate action, the SDGs have opened many doors for partnerships that draw on diverse insights and expertise.

Organizations like the World Economic Forum also contribute by creating platforms for dialogue among leaders from various sectors. Their annual meetings in Davos bring together heads of state, business leaders, and thinkers to discuss critical global issues and explore collaborative solutions. These gatherings highlight how a shared commitment can spark innovative ideas and actionable strategies to tackle complex challenges.

As we step into this new era, we must also recognize the importance of cultural exchange and inclusivity. A global narrative that promotes growth should include voices from marginalized communities, ensuring the benefits of progress reach everyone. This effort is urgent. Historically, technological advancements have often favored those who are already privileged, leaving vulnerable populations behind. To shape a future defined by fairness, we must actively seek out and amplify the voices of those who have been overlooked, making sure they are included in conversations about innovation and progress.

In practical terms, fostering inclusivity in our movement requires a commitment to engage with a variety of communities. Initiatives like community-led forums and collaborative design processes can create spaces for marginalized groups to share their insights. For example, programs like "Design Thinking Workshops" invite people from different backgrounds to work together on local problems. By giving these individuals a chance to contribute their ideas, we can develop more comprehensive and effective strategies tailored to the needs of the communities we want to serve.

Technology can also play a crucial role in bridging gaps in accessibility and participation. Digital platforms can enable collaboration across distances, allowing voices from every corner of the globe to join the discussion. Social media campaigns and online forums can highlight stories from individuals who have been historically excluded from decision-making. By leveraging technology, we can open up the conversation about growth and create an inclusive narrative that truly reflects the hopes and dreams of all people.

As we work toward this shared vision, it's important to paint a hopeful picture of the future that resonates with everyone. Imagine a world where technological advancements not only enhance global cooperation and shared prosperity but also show a deep commitment to the greater good. Picture a future where innovations in renewable energy help combat climate change, where healthcare improvements ensure that everyone has access to essential services, and where education empowers future generations with the skills they need to thrive in a changing world.

This vision isn't just a pipe dream; it's an attainable goal that demands collective action. Building a global community requires inspiring individuals to see themselves as active participants in this movement. By sharing stories of successful partnerships, we can spark enthusiasm and encourage others to join in. For instance, the success of the Ellen MacArthur Foundation's Circular Economy 100, which brings together leading companies, governments, and universities to promote a circular economy, demonstrates how a shared vision and action can lead to real change.

In this effort, we need to keep a sense of urgency and hope alive. The challenges we face may seem overwhelming, but they are not impossible to overcome. As we unite to create a brighter future, we must remember that even small actions can lead to significant change. Individuals and communities can engage in grassroots initiatives, while organizations can adopt policies that prioritize sustainability and inclusivity. By nurturing a spirit of collaboration and embracing a shared vision, we can together navigate the complexities of our world, turning challenges into opportunities.

The journey toward a limitless future isn't merely a destination; it's an active and united process. By coming together with a shared vision and purpose, we can break down the barriers that separate us and tap into the full potential of growth. Collaboration across sectors, forming global alliances, lifting up marginalized voices, and articulating a shared vision for the future are all critical pieces of this movement.

As we stand at this pivotal moment in history, the invitation is clear: let's unite, embrace our shared humanity, and strive for a future rich with promise and possibility. The time to act is now, and a better tomorrow awaits those who are willing to dream, work together, and move toward a limitless future.

Conclusion

As we reach the end of this manifesto, it's clear that the path forward is not just a possibility – it's a necessity. The principles of Effective Accelerationism offer us a roadmap to navigate the complexities of our rapidly changing world. By embracing innovation and harnessing the power of technology, we can transform challenges into opportunities.

Throughout this book, we've explored how stagnation threatens our progress and how acceleration can propel us towards a brighter future. From AI and robotics to renewable energy and space exploration, the potential for positive change is immense. But this potential can only be realized if we act with purpose and determination.

The choice is yours. Will you remain a passive observer, or will you become an active participant in shaping our collective destiny? Every breakthrough, every innovation, every step forward begins with individuals who dare to dream big and act boldly.

Remember, you are not alone in this journey. Across the globe, pioneers and visionaries are already putting these ideas into action. Join them. Be part of the movement that will define the next chapter of human history.

The future is not something that happens to us – it's something we create. Let's accelerate towards it, together.

Cornel Jefferson

www.ingramcontent.com/pod-product-compliance
Lightning Source LLC
Chambersburg PA
CBHW052150220526
45471CB00004B/1607